STUCK

Where I Was Last Hurt

ISBN: 978-1-83556-082-2 - PAPERBACK

ISBN: 978-1-83556-083-9 - HARDBACK

ISBN: 978-1-83556-084-6 - EBOOK

Book Design by HMDPUBLISHING

CONTENTS

PREFACE

It's been 7 seven years, since I published *1177: Undaunted (Undaunted)*. Soon after I finished it, I began working on *Stuck*. Which was, then, titled *8194;* the month and year I started at Cookman. Initially, my intentions were to continue documenting my journey where I left off. *8194* would have been a chronological depiction of college life and young adulthood. The work would have been filled with occurrences and instances but void of substance. So, I put it away.

My long-awaited love had finally come. I no longer needed anything, accept him. I was engrossed. I was so consumed with him that I didn't notice me. I forgot me. I lost me. I only saw what he saw, in me. My internalization of his depictions had morphed me into a person I no longer recognized. Or maybe I did. Maybe I was finally seeing what I'd been carrying around for decades. And what people saw when they encountered me. A little girl. The 5-year-old Charkes that was neglected. The 7-year-old Charkes that was molested. The 12-year-old Charkes that was never affirmed. The 17-year-old Charkes that was hurt. And now, the 45-year-old Charkes that is stuck where she was last hurt.

Stuck is an open letter to me. It is me writing through my life's repetitious cycles and asking why I kept ending up in the same place. HURT. As I lived, and then wrote, there was one common factor-my temperament. My personality. The consistent feedback about my disposition forced me to think carefully about how I showed up. I wanted to understand how people experienced me and why. And the realization of that ruminating period is what you're holding in your hands.

My hope is that my letter causes you to write your own letter. A letter that would reveal your place of *Stuck*. At which point, you'll release where you've been to go where you need to be.

I HAD TO GO

Glassy with tears, my eyes glanced at every tree that sat along Interstate 95 (I95). It wasn't that I was suddenly interested in botany-it's just what happens when you are in deep thought. Your brain makes you superficially focus on something while you think about something else. Only minutes had passed since I'd left home, and I was saddened by thoughts of what would happen to them in my absence. How would they survive? Who would cook, clean and wash their clothes? Had India and Simone watched me closely enough to know what to do? Were they up to filling my shoes? And how would the boys respond to them? All unanswered questions that pained me to my core. I wanted to turn around and go back home but knew I couldn't. Because staying in Miami, in the projects, would not benefit me or them. I had to do better for all of us. And then my tears dried.

By the time we'd gotten to Daytona Beach (Florida), my heart was racing with anticipation. Kevin exited I-95 to International Speedway Boulevard and about 2 miles in, there it was! THE sign! The sign that had greeted millions of people before me but went unnoticed. But for me, it was like my first car. It was like a boy I'd fallen in love with. It was new. "Welcome to Daytona" it read. And although we passed it swiftly, I could still see it miles after. I see it now.

Our first stop was "Checkers". We went there because it sat conveniently on the corner of Martin Luther King Boulevard and International Speedway-walking distance from Bethune-Cookman's main campus. I'd requested a checker burger with cheese combo, but Sherrae insisted that cheese cost too much and had me settle for a burger without it. Adults are strange like that. What difference would 18 cents make to your budget? I was annoyed but quickly got over it because I had much more to think about than my sister's frugal ways.

Our next stop was the Moore Gymnasium-"The Gym". This is where my acceptance letter directed me for registration and my class schedule. Kevin parked his SUV among the many other cars in the gym's parking lot. The sight of the gym itself caused excitement I hadn't experienced since I went to Spain. I was finally here, the place where I'd start my new life. The gym was an old appearing maroon and white colored brick building, in need of a paint job. And to the back of it was a huge grassy field-an area I would soon become very familiar with. We walked up a short set of stairs that led to what we found was a back door. But it was locked. Re-directed by onlookers, we walked around to the front of the gym. As soon as I passed the front double doors, my nose was filled with the scent of stale moths-like the aroma that exuded from your great-grandmother's dresser drawers. The walls were adorned with framed pictures of former athletes. Some hung crookedly. Every step of the way we were greeted by a variety of folk, smiling from ear to ear. "Welcome to Cookman." "Welcome, Wildcats!" With each smiling face, I grew more eager to see what college was all about. I was ready.

I'd never seen anything like it before. There were people every-where and the noise was deafening, sort of like walking into a night-club. We stood at the door and looked around until we could figure out what was going on. And although they were hard to see amongst all the people, there were signs and lines. One line for registration, one for class schedules and the other for book vouchers. Finally, I fought through the confusion, registered and got my class schedule. And not to my surprise, my daily trips to the park (while I was sup-posed to be at school) had caught up with me. I had remedial math and reading. But that didn't matter. There was nothing I could do about it except to take my ass to class and pass.

I was assigned to Lee Hall. It was one of the trifecta of dorms, a good distance away from the yard where the majority of the dorms were located. The other two were Moore and Thompson Hall. Of the three, Thompson Hall was the only boys' dorm.

The rooms were set up as suites and each suite suited four people-two per room. All four people shared a bathroom that separated each of the rooms. There were no other dorms set up this way. It was said that the "Trifecta" was reserved for students who had the best academic performance in high school. I was a little confused about why I was assigned to Lee Hall as I'd graduated from Braddock with a 1.9 g.p.a. and my remedial Math and English courses proved that I hadn't been the crem-dela-crem in high school.

Sherrae and I excitedly decorated my room. My summer job at the local grocery store had afforded me (what I thought) were the prettiest navy blue and white window valances and matching bedspread. I'd accessorized with navy blue throw rugs. My (maternal) grandmother had let me borrow her miniature refrigerator. I didn't realize she'd let me borrow it until I went home for a break, and she asked that I return it. I was floored, but not surprised, as she didn't have a relationship with me or my siblings. Its non-existence reflected the relationship she had with my mother. For reasons that are not totally clear to me, their relationship was stormy, and I imagine both she and my mother's "I don't give two fucks" attitude contributed to the tension.

I also brought the microwave we had at home. Before packing it, I had to clean it. This included removing its backing to clear all the roaches that lived inside. Our house was a roach habitat, so it's only natural that they infest everything within the house - especially warm dark areas. It would have been ideal to purchase a new one, but it was out of my summer budget. I couldn't afford it. I could only hope that I'd cleared the microwave of all the "brown boys" so that my room would not become inundated with them.

After I was settled in, Sherrae and Kevin headed back home. Neither of them seemed to be sad or worried about leaving me alone. I guess because I'd always been independent, they were confident I'd be ok. Sherrae handed me $100.00 and Kevin lectured me about boys, boys and more boys. I hugged them both, turned around and walked away into my new life.

My roommate had finally arrived. Hailing from Jacksonville, Florida, she stood about 5 feet tall and had dark chocolate skin and wide hips. She had what Bahamians refer to as gun cases. The reference compares a woman's wide hips to that of a man wearing hip gun holders. They were as wide as mine are now as a grown woman.

Her teeth left a lot to be desired. The bottom row looked as if someone just threw them in her mouth without care about where they landed. And when she spoke, every vowel was drawn out—like she was from Texas. Although we didn't spend a lot of time together, our brief conversations proved we didn't have much in common. I wasn't sure anyone would have much in common with me. I mean, I'd been sexually molested, verbally and physically abused, raised seven kids and had a mother who was homeless. Shit, by the time I'd gotten to college, I'd lived the life of an adult. So, it would be quite difficult for other girls my age to relate. Well, at least that's what I thought.

For some reason, my time in the room with "Little Ms. Duval" was short-lived. I ended up changing rooms and roommates. Lee Hall, room 219 was my destination for the year and my newest "room doom" was named Alice. Unlike my first roommate, Alice and I hit it off, instantly. She was a light-skinned cutie who had come to Bethune-Cookman (BCC), via Leesburg, Florida but was from Detroit, Michigan. Alice was chunky and full of energy. Her teeth were white like chicklet gum and were accentuated by a deep left cheek dimple. We were as thick as thieves. When you saw her, you saw me, except when I went to the cafeteria (the cafe). Alice thought the cafe's food was horrible. So, she opted out and settled for "Checkers", "The Grill" or whatever snacks she brought from the food store. Little did she know, the cafe was about much more than the food. It was a social place. It was where you met up with your boo or where you found a boo. Where you meet up with your dawgs and where you learn the infamous BCC prayer:

> *"Christ is the head of this house, the unforeseen guest at every meal, the silent listener of every conversation. Amen."*

Those arriving early to the café were expected and directed to re-cite that prayer- out loud. You could be dead in the middle of walking to your favorite table, with your favorite people, with a tray of food in hand and someone would say, Uhnt-uhh, we need to pray". And without a countdown, we'd belt it out, in unison.

Despite the great time I was having, I thought of my siblings-often. I wondered what they were up to. I thought about the ones that were attending school when I left, and wondered if they were staying on track. I was also concerned about how much further off track the most vulnerable ones were. Had they gotten into trouble? Had they succumbed to the dope man or become dope men themselves? India would write me letters from time to time, updating me on what was going on with her and grieving about Trea, Chaz and Eddie's insubordination. Those letters would draw me in-pull at my heart strings and cause me to call Babalu to see what was happening. He'd offer the same grievances and "tell" me that I needed to talk to the girls too because they weren't listening to him either. But their lives were out of my direct control. There was nothing a call could do. They needed my presence. That which I could not give. I'd then fold Inia's letter and reconnect the phone's base and receiver, after talking to Babalu, in grief, but determined to stay the course in my new life.

CHAPTER 2

SCHOOLIN' LIFE

My first year at Cookman was seamless. I immediately tested out of those remedial courses, putting me back on a four-year college plan. I decided to major in nursing. My decision wasn't based on me knowing any nurses or being impressed with the profession. I just knew it to be safe. Getting and keeping a job was important because there were more than a few people depending on me back home. Nursing was also a step above my childhood aspiration of being a waitress. I used to watch the T.V. show "Mel's Diner" as a child. I was drawn in and enamored with the show after the first episode. The uniforms and the way Mel would say, "Dingy, get the lead out." and when Flo would say, "Mel, kiss my grits." made me want to be a waitress. The cast appeared happy, and the women didn't take Mel's shit. Well, all except for Vera. In hindsight, "serving" is likely what made the show and profession attractive to me.

I also got to go to Black College Reunion (BCR) during my first year at Cookman. Hot Damn!! BCR was basically "Young black folk take over Daytona Beach's beach line for the entire weekend." And it was fucking amazing. Alice and I were strapped for cash, so we crashed in our boys' room. They didn't mind because rooms were only used for showering and changing clothes and even that was in the wee hours of the morning. The event was epic. There were black teenagers and young adults all over the place drinking, smoking, and dancing - having a blast. Most would tirelessly walk the strip while others slow-rode their cars on the main street. The girls wore close to nothing. Ass cheeks, stretchmarks and titties were in abundance. And the skimpier the outfit, the more you were noticed-which was more than important to our young simple asses back then. The guys would sashay around shirtless. And if you were an Omega, you would only need to wear a pair of purple, omega-embellished bikini underwear and gold boots. I couldn't believe what I was seeing. I mean, living in Miami was an experience within itself…drive-bys, crackheads, and bowling ball paint jobs, but experiencing BCR was different. The people, the music, the vibes, the freedom-CRAZY! Suddenly, I was a bird that had finally found life outside of its cage.

I took College Algebra and English, African American History, Religion and Freshman Seminar. They were easier than the courses I'd taken only months prior. Freshman seminar was especially easy. It was a requirement for all college nubies. I never understood the intent of the course though. It seemed like something the school's leadership put together without much thought. We'd gather in the college's chapel, adorned in our bright green plastic sun-visors that read "Crab" across the front. They were given out during our first week of school. It was a way to separate classes-making freshmen distinct from everyone else. And they were required for attendance credit. Freshman seminar presenters would include our beloved president at the time-Oswald Perry Bronson (Dr. Bronson). This was the time when we first heard "My Friends". It was Dr. Bronson's signature salutation and the way we would always remember him. Even in passing him by on campus, we would greet him with "My Friends"-sometimes catching him when he would say it-finishing in unison.

Freshman Seminar didn't have a syllabus, assignment, or home-work-we only had to show up and wear those ugly ass green sun visors. Outside of Dr. Bronson, the presenters would either bore you to death or have you sitting at the edge of your seat with ex-citement. The latter would always occur when The Concert Cho-rale performed. A girl that would become one of my closest friends was a member-Moe. Concert Chorale would perform and sang their butts off but if "Order My Steps" wasn't a part of the performance, baby, the audience would chant-" Order My Steps, Order My Steps", begging Moe to sing. Seriously, you would hear hundreds of students stomping, clapping and yelling the song's title. This would go on until Moe stepped out from the group and on to the front of the stage with microphone in hand. It was Moe's and the chorale's signature piece. Her voice was just as sweet as she was (and still is). The song's lyrics represent who I knew her to be then and now.

> "Humbly I ask Thee, teach me your will. While you are working, help me be still. For Satan is busy, God is real. Order my steps in your word. Please, order my steps in your word."

Moe's soprano voice would resonate through the room. She was only about 5'3", but her presence and voice were grand. Accompanied by her peers in song and dance, she'd well every eye in attendance. And it didn't matter how many times she performed that song. We had the same response. "Please, order my steps in your word".

I love you, Mo.

I was sitting in LLC's lobby "shooting the breeze" when I heard the announcement. It went something like this:

> "Ladies, if you're interested in joining the 14kt. Gold Dance Team, tryouts will be held next Monday. Meet at the band field dressed in a white T-shirt, black tights and black V-cut shorts and ready to work."

I was hyped. I hadn't danced since I left Miami, and until that moment, I wasn't aware of any campus dance activities. This was my chance to do what I loved most. DANCE! I wasn't afraid, because my training at Inner City Children's Touring Dance (ICCTDC) Company precluded skill as reason for declination. My sisters and I joined the company five years prior. We were introduced to the company's founder and owner, Florene Lithcutt-Nichols, by Sister Shirley. She was a minister that live close by and had taken us in as her "God-sent children". She took care of us, and many others, like her own. Sister Shirley's one and only child, Jett, danced for Ms. Nichols when she was our age. So, she knew, firsthand, how getting us connected with Ms. Nichols would affect our lives, then and in times to come.

Meeting Sister Shirley and Ms. Nichols literally turned my world around. Through Sister Shirley, I learned God and the Christian religion. I learned to praise and worship, witnessed and had the Holy Ghost and got acquainted with, what I later learned, was extra virgin olive oil. Sister Shirley would anoint our heads with it before major prayer and prophesy. She continues these practices to date. If I go and visit her now, she'll surely have a stash prepared-poured into a small plastic bottle. And yes, I use it. We all need something extraordinary to get through "Life Itself".

Sister Shirley set the foundation for what is now my spiritual life. Making that connection early on has gotten me through a great deal of challenges. It taught me that my humanness does not provide all answers. And at times, it is flawed, depressed, unsure, and haughty. All of which causes me to believe less or too much of myself, driving poor decision-making. But when I just "be", get quiet, and allow God to whisper in that silence, I draw from his strength and my life unfolds in ways that are incomparable to when I draw from myself.

I often think of what my life would've been like without Sister Shirley. Would I know God-as I do? Would I ever have met Ms. Nichols? What would have happened with my middle school prom? Would I have gone? Sister Shirley made sure I went. She got me the cutest white dress from Syms department store. It was covered in lace and secured around my neck-allowing a little back-out action. And the finishing touches were the elbow length laced gloves that she allowed to slouch around my wrists. Jett did my hair. She frenched rolled it and created little curls at the corners, near my ears, dropping at the top of my cheek bones. She added a touch of make-up-using rose colored lipstick to highlight my skinny little cheeks-giving my young face flare. And I can't forget the stockings we, last minute, got from Zayres. It was only a half block away from Sister Shirley's house on 54th street. While they seem insignificant, compared to the rest of my outfit, they were a big deal to me. They were white and embezzled with stones and extra knitting extending from my ankles to my calves. In sort of a zig-zag pattern. I felt like a princess. And for the first time, I felt pretty. There's a picture of me posing in Sister Shirley's' dad's Cadillac, outside her house. My eyes and smile convey what I'm feeling. Happiness. It's one of the pictures I often refer to when I'm not feeling well. When my humanness takes over and sadness wants to settle. I look at the picture and ask myself, "what would little Keese do"? "Do you remember how strong she was?" "You remember how little she worried and how much she pressed on"? Then I start to get my shit together.

Ms. Nichols provided the social and artistic exposure I needed. Because of her (and Sister Shirley), I was able to perform at The World's Fair, in Seville, Spain. I write about this experience, in detail, in my first book- "*1177:Undaunted*". The trip caused many "Ah-Ha" moments. And the most galvanizing was the importance of exposure. Sister Shirley gave me God and Ms. Nichols. Ms. Nichols gave me dance and confidence. Dance and confidence gave me hope. And hope gave me a future. A future that includes me writing to and for you.

Monday had finally arrived. I was ready, on time, dressed and stretched. Although I don't recall how many girls accompanied me during tryouts, I remember HIM and HER. He was a young man, androgynous and grand. His walk, talk and presence made it apparent that he was a dancer. His hair was jet black, soft appearing and combed to the back. There was a shadow of a mustache adorning his top lip. His arms were toned, and his feet slightly turned when he walked. You couldn't help but notice him. He walked with a sway, threw "shade" when someone looked "off" and moved with precision.

She was a dark-skinned girl who looked to be older than a member of the dance team should have been. She had about 20 inches of dark weave that was pulled back and made full by the baseball cap that adorned her head. She had bulgy eyes-sort of like people who suffered from severe forms of hyperthyroidism. She did not have the body of a dancer. She was thick and pudgy in the middle. I gave her the benefit of the doubt though. Back at home, Trisha was as thick as they come but could move like melted butter. Trisha was a better dancer than I was, so size is clearly relative. She welcomed us and introduced herself as the captain of the team, "The 14Kt Gold Dancers". I was oblivious to who these dancers were and what the name meant, but I would soon find out.

After introductions, she took a backseat, and he took over. We stretched, and 30 minutes later, we were learning choreography. Guided by "Pure Love" (Ce-Ce Peneston), I melted back into the space that gave me freedom. I was happy and peaceful all at the same time. The choreography made the time even more momentous. It was sexy, technical and fun-much like him. I feel like dancing just thinking about it. Once we had the piece down, we were asked to perform individually. And chile... I couldn't wait for my turn. I stood mid-field and waited for him to count. "5, 6, 5678", and I went the fuck off. I smiled when I needed to, and duck lipped and side-eyed when appropriate. My toes were pointed, my chin was up, and my back was straight. I could see them out of the corner of my eyes looking with amusement. Like, "Damn, dis bitch can dance. Way da fuck she come from?" And when I was done, I walked back to my spot in line, winded, but confident.

As with any other audition, they told us they'd let us know who made it-at a later date. With the technical training I'd gotten from ICCTDC and how experienced a performer I was, I knew I'd killed it. And a week later, I got the news. I had become a "preliminary" 14Kt Gold Dancer who was also, I might add, a part of the "Baddest Band in The Land" The Marching Wildcats of Bethune Cookman College. I'll explain the "preliminary" shit later. Those reading this who were a part of our band, or any black college band, know what that status means.

CHAPTER 3:

SUMMER 95

O k, ok. I left out an important part of my freshman year. I forgot to mention when and where I met Mr. Osborne. Ron Christopher Osborne, that is. He was a sophomore from Jacksonville, FL, and as so many students did, he was hanging out in LLC, in the computer lab, doing homework. LLC's computer lab was the highlight of our dorm and the thing that set our accommodations apart from others. I guess it was a reward for being the scholars we were. Other students would either use their own PCs or use the ones in the campus library. The ones you had to wait on during crunch times. You know, when papers were due or when seniors were on the countdown-which also involved a major paper. One would wait hours for a computer to free up. Over time, I was appreciative of the convenience and resources LLC afforded me.

One night I happened to be in the computer lab at the same time as Ron, and the rest was history.

Ron stood over 6 feet tall, had paper bag brown skin and oddly large hands. His dress was more than eccentric, including the nose ring in his left nostril. He drove a doo-doo brow stick shift, of an unknown make and model, that looked to be on its last leg. Ron was also one of the Marching Wildcats' drum majors. He was unlike any guy I'd experienced, favored or dated back home. Miami guys were (and still are) the same. They looked alike, dressed alike and spoke the same words. No individuality, except when it came to comparing themselves to other cities. And that comparison always made them the "hardest niggahs" in the world. That was a huge turn-off for me. So, meeting and experiencing Ron was a breath of fresh air. His unconventional style was magnetic. And he was extremely intelligent. His mind matched mine. Intellect was necessary for Charkes' law of attraction. You can be fine as hell, but if you dumb as bricks, I will give you the cold shoulder like a gold digger when a broke niggah approaches her (Jermaine Cole). It starts with the mind. I must be mentally stimulated to be wholly attracted to you. A beautiful mind can minimize the most significant physical imperfections. And Ron had (and still does) have a beautiful mind.

My outward look of normalcy had most stuck on why I would be with such a guy. Or-how he could lock down a woman like me. While I understand the queries, to know me is to know why I was so attracted to Ron. And why we fell in love.

Ron and I hit it off immediately, and after that night, Ron are I started going together. We stayed that way for 3 years.

My freshman year came and went. I passed all my classes with As and Bs and was excited to return home to my brothers and sisters and ICCTDC. I landed a much-needed summer job in the city, off 62nd street, near the post office, with Kevin's boss Sam Holloway. Mr. Holloway had a private security business and needed some administrative assistance at the time. I answered phones, filed papers and made sure checks were disbursed on Fridays. Kevin would drop me off and pick me up every day. He was awesome like that. Mr. Holloway paid me seven bucks an hour, working full time. This was more than enough to buy the laundry list of items required for band camp: white "Arab" T-shirts, "V" cut shorts-in multiple colors, sneakers, and socks.

The job was simple, which made it boring. I mean, it doesn't take a rocket scientist to answer phones and file papers. Mr. Holloway was the most interesting part of the job. I guess his personality provided me with daily doses of amusement. He was a big black guy-almost blue-black-that stood about 6'1" and could've possibly been taller had it not been for the kyphosis that had started to set in. His face was round and full of jet-black hair. His crown was just as black, and wavy. It was natural. He didn't need to use "Murray's" or "Sportin Waves", wear a wave cap at night, or spend hours brushing his hair like "Chicago" on Poetic Justice.

Mr. Holloway's face kind of sagged, giving him a permanent frown, and made him look like a bulldog. He always spoke slowly, without inflexion and in a direct manner. You never walked away from a conversation with him misunderstanding. As an adult, I've learned to appreciate people who communicate the way Mr. Holloway did. Not only because it's the way I communicate, but also because it mitigates the bullshit involved in relating to people. There is no pretense or fluff to sort through-just straight Hennessey, no chaser.

At least three times a week Mr. Holloway would buy lunch, which was perfect for me. His generosity allowed me to save more money for the upcoming school year. I'd already set in my mind how much I had to spend on practice clothes but wasn't sure about what my other costs would be. Uniforms were foreseen, but I didn't know if they would be as expensive as the ones I wore for ICCTDC performances. Come to think of it, I didn't pay one red cent for those uniforms. Ms. Nichols took care of everything. So, what the hell am I talking about? LOL.

Who ever was hustling food in the area would get Mr. Holloway's money. Most times it was a little old Haitian lady pushing a wheeled, metal laundry basket full of BBQ chicken and vegetable rice. The food was contained in white styrofoam and stacked tight and high. The dish was basic but would be fresh, piping hot and seasoned to perfection. Mr. Holloway enjoyed it. He'd sit with his head lowered so that his mouth was close to the plate. This made it easier to get to the food. And not a crumb would be left behind. We sat across from each other, so I was able to watch him while I ate. His eating was comparable to synchronous swimming. "Pick-up, chew, swallow", all in one breath. Shit, I don't think he remembered to breathe while he was eating. It was more than interesting to watch.

There was another gentleman who worked for Mr. Holloway. Mr. Roberts. I never knew his first name and never asked. Out of respect, I would never call him by it, so there was no use in the query. Mr. Holloway called him "Old Man". It was fitting literally and figuratively. To this day, his role in the company is unknown to me. My guess is that he managed the security officers. I would also guess that he and Mr. Holloway were close friends, like family, and he was given the job to keep busy.

"Old Man" sticks out in my memories because he was the first person to explain the difference between "Love" and "In Love ". You see, Old Man was married. And although he loved his wife of 50 years, he was in love with another woman. He spoke of his wife in a respectful and formal manner. But when he spoke of the other woman, his eyes lit up. Like a kid's eyes on Christmas Eve. With joy, Mr. Roberts would describe their rendezvous in New York. It's where she lived. He'd go and on about their Central Park walks, and late-night coffee runs-when they would talk for hours at a time. Old Man loved his wife but was in love with someone else. I honestly felt too young, in age, and in relation to Old Man for such conversations. But I rolled with it. I always thought he needed someone to tell. Someone to share the conflict of his mind and heart with, so that he didn't feel so heavy. Burdened. Given what I understand about relationships now, his wife knew. I assume she weighed her options and opted to stay. Being married to someone for 50 years is no easy flight and jumping off the plane is senseless, especially that late in the trip (in some situations). As I write this, my mind wonders, creating an ending to their story. Hopefully, Old Man and his wife remained married sans his mistress. I also hope his mistress found the everlasting love she sought with Old Man and within herself.

That same summer, l helped Ms. Nichols with the company. She was preparing for the summer recital and could use the extra hands. She'd asked me to teach the babies and assist with the ins and outs of the recital. I'd owed her half of my life, so there was no question in helping her. By this time, the studio had suffered roof damage, so we were practicing in Miami Northwestern Senior High's (The West) auditorium (the old building). A new school has been built since.

In addition to helping with the kids, Ms. Nichols asked me to perform a piece as Josephine Baker. She thought I was perfect for the part, saying I looked and moved just like her. I don't believe I'd cut my hair by that time, so Ms. Nichols' comparison was more about movement than looks. I was a soft dancer. Not in effort but in motion. I think it's because of my body's habitus. I wasn't muscular and was barely toned. So, these physical characteristics showed up in my way of dancing. Soft, like liquid.

Playing Josephine Baker was important for many reasons. She was integral in Women's History, African American History, Civil Rights History and Art History. Her performances meant black girls from southern North America could take basic dance and song and make it revolutionary. Josephine consciously entertained audiences all over the world and used the stage as leverage to further societal change. She became one of African America's most powerful voices. I was proud to portray her.

Ms. Nichols had two sons. One of them, Apon, was a performer in a local Miami Dance Group-Live in Color (LIC). LIC was also comprised of Zedric ((Zed)Founder), Van and Devon. Later, I became aware of members that were active prior to me meeting Apon. But by the time I came to know LIC, only Zed, Apon, Van and Devon were actively dancing.

LIC wasn't your "usual" Miami booty shakin group. These knee-grows could fucking dance. Technically. They could leap, jump, split and arabesque like trained ballerinas. And at the same time, they would sit in a squat for 60 seconds while thrusting their arms back and forth and around. Their talent was raw and comparable to the likes of Alvin Ailey and Arthur Mitchell. Zed was the lead dancer and choreographer. He combined booty-shakin with modern and jazz-styled dance, creating what he now calls "Urban Funk". Everyone loved LIC. Girls waited for them to either gyrate to Luke's "I Wanna Rock" or roll and dry hump the stage to Silk's "Lose Control"-which was my personal favorite. And their costumes just added to the flavor. Zed's mom, Ms. Shelia, would design and sew them all.

They'd always be colorful and fun-loud green, loud pink, red, yellow, purple-you name it, they wore it.

I met Zed during my freshman year in high school. Ms. Nichols added hip-hop to our repertoire and Zed was our instructor. I would say that I was an "average" Hip-Hop dancer. As mentioned earlier, my body wasn't ideal. I was thin and lacked physical definition, causing me to glide through movement as opposed to striking movement. In turn, my execution wasn't as aesthetically pleasing as one with a more toned, developed body. I knew this well before performing any of Zed's pieces. Remember, I'm a native of Liberty City and we've made a decent contribution to hip-hop, including dance. "The Wiggle", "Creep Dog", "Throw Da D" (and "P") and our most famous, "Doo-Doo Brown"-all of which I'd tried (while alone, in my bedroom, in front of a mirror) but didn't quite look like the girls I'd see at "The Jams"-which were pop-up block parties thrown by legendary "Sugar Hill" DJ, Uncle Al.

Uncle Al would show up on the corner of 15th avenue and 71st street, stack 8 speakers, in sets of two, and make a wall that was at least 7 feet high. He would announce his presence with song and the beckoning of his voice. Every jam session was like a performance. The songs he played were Miami's late 80s and early 90s Hip Hop hits like "Pick It Up", J.T. Money's "Hoe Problems" or "Keep Dancing". But these songs, alone, didn't compare to Al's ad-libs. The shit he would say while the instrumental of "Bass Rock" or Barry White's "Together Brothers" theme played in the background seemed more meaningful than the extraordinary hits that accompanied his voice. His alto utterance saying, "Slip-Slide -Ride, Slip-Slide-Ride, Slip-Slide-Ride, Oooh-Whats Up, Santa Claus Comin-Santa Claus Comin-Santa Claus Comin, To the Break -Don't Stop, Ride-Ride-Slide, Slip-Slide-Ride, Slip-Slide-Ride, Ooooh, Don't Stop" put everyone in a trance. The crowd danced to Al's beat, not Barry's. He was at the cutting edge of disc jockeying. He was before his time. And had he still been alive today, he'd stand in the ranks with DJ Cassidy, DJ Scratch, Grand Wizard Theodore and DJ Premiere. Rest In Peace, Uncle Al.

LIC spawned sub-groups-Live in Color Ladies (LICL) and Future Live in Color (FLIC). While LIC was comprised of adult men, LICL was made up of adult women. And FLIC was made up of a group of fine-ass teenage boys! As a girl, I was always in love. At first sight of an attractive boy, I'd planned our wedding, knew what our babies would look like, how I would serve him, and how we would live out the rest of our lives-happily ever after.

I'd fallen for 2 of FLIC's members Ron and T. T was fair-skinned and thin but muscular and edgy. He wore his hair locked and when he danced, you'd notice his hair before his moves. T was the guy all the girls from Liberty City liked. He represented the young rough necks we were used to. The ones that stood in front of your house or on the corner selling weed or notifying the weed seller that police, referred to as "9", were nearby. I assume this abbreviation came about because 9 was the first number in 911. The notification would go something like this, "9 in the hole"-meaning the police were within feet of the drug hole. Or "9 on 75 22"- meaning the police were on 75th street and 22nd Avenue. Either way, you needed to get out of the hole and store your weed, crack, or cocaine where the police couldn't' find it or link it to you. Or your ass was goin straight to the county or TGK.

T's face was chiseled like a grown man. And so was his body. He was also relatable, to me at least. He'd lost both of his parents, years prior, so his uncle on his dad's side took him in. Despite being a part of FLIC, T got into trouble with the law. I was empathetic to this. I understood. My brothers suffered in the same way. Parental absence is a major factor in childhood growth and development. And the earlier the absence, the earlier retardation. T and I talked a couple of time on the phone, but he knew he wasn't good for me. So, he fell back. Meaning, he left me alone. My heartbreak was short lived because I had my eye on Ron too.

Ron was a fair-skinned, skinny guy with a pudge nose and a baby face. He lived in the Norland/Carol City area-near what was then, "Joe Robbie" stadium. It's now called "Hard Rock" stadium. Ron was shy. You saw it in his eyes and in his voice when he spoke to you.

But when he would perform with LIC, he was a different person. The gyratin and pumpin took him from Ron to Rondario!

Ron and I kinda-sorta dated for a spell. Nothing major, mainly phone conversations. Once, he invited me to dinner at his house. I was living with Sherrae and Kevin at the time, in Sherrae's mom's house. Somehow, I'd convinced them to let me go. Sherrae was (and still is) a softie, so she deferred to Kevin's decision. Kevin was old school. He was a protector. So, his allowance came with stipulations. He had to drop me off and pick me up and I could only stay for 3 hours. I didn't care though. I'd gotten a chance to spend time with the guy I'd daydreamed about for months.

It was a brisk Sunday afternoon and there wasn't a cloud in the sky. Well, I hadn't noticed any. (I honestly don't remember what the weather was that day. But this is my story, so it's going to be the most beautifullest day ever!) Sherrae's mom was living in Miami Lakes, so our trip to Ron's didn't take long. I was nervous and excited all at the same time. My hair was pulled back in a homemade bun. Before H&M got the "lick" on the plastic doughnut-looking buns that spoke the last words of, "buy me", before check-out, the girls in the hood made them. We'd take a black scrunch sock, cut it across the toe, and roll it into a doughnut like shape. By this time, we'd already brushed our hair back into a tight ponytail, securing its slickness with Pink Moisturizer and black Prostyle styling gel. The sock bun would be placed around the ponytail and then the free hair would be raked over, covering the bun in its entirety. The last piece of the process involved placing a scrunchie around the bun, covering the hair that had been raked around. My hair-do modeled that of a ballerina getting ready to preform Swan Lake. It was perfect.

I believe I wore a "short set" that day. A short set is an outfit that required an exact matching bottom and top-by color and design. For teenagers like me, short sets were the most worn outfits. They could be purchased cheaply. They were comfortable. And they were "in". Although I don't remember the details of the outfit, it had to pass the "Kevin" test-loose, long enough, and age-appropriate. Otherwise, I wasn't going anywhere.

We arrived. As I got out of the car, Kevin gave me one last glance, looked into the whites of my eyes and told me to be ready to go in exactly 2 hours and 59 minutes. I smiled in agreement, but in my head, I was like "This dude is impossible. I can't ever do shit." As I closed the car door, Ron opened his front door-a sign that he had been anxiously and excitedly anticipating my arrival. LOL. Well, at least that's what I'm telling myself now. We both greeted each other with smiles. He beckoned me inside by moving out of the door-way. I stepped into his living room, and immediately felt warm and comfortable. I also felt pressed for time. I only had 1 hour and 50 minutes to lay down the moves that would secure my "happily ever after".

Ron took me into what appeared to be his family room. There sat his mother and father. They both looked too old to have been parents to a teenager-looking more like his grandparents. Each of them waved, smiled and quickly turned their attention back to the television show they were watching before I'd gotten there. Now I know you're waiting to see what happened during my visit. And here it is-NOTHING! We ate dinner, had some superficial conversations, and watched television. And all this activity occurred while I was in one chair and he in the other. The entire time I wondered why he hadn't sat closer to me. Why hadn't he kissed me or even held my hand? I guess my Misty Copeland bun and Brenda Jenkins (from "227) outfit wasn't working, cause our date did not go as expected. Shit, I just knew we'd be planning our next date and what college we'd attend-because we couldn't bear the thought of not being with one another. But there wasn't even a whisper of what I'd envisioned. Kevin had finally come to pick me up, and I was more than sad that I had nothing to feel guilty about. I didn't have anything to hide from him or lie about. So, when he asked me "How did it go", my response of "Ok" was exactly what I meant.

While lying on the floor of Sherrae and Kevin's apartment, the front door opened, and Kevin appeared. Standing near my head, Kevin says excitedly, "Charkes, I have a surprise for you." I'm like, "OK". I wasn't excited. Like most middle-class couples, Kevin and Sherrae lived humbly. So, I knew I wasn't getting a car, my own apartment or a wad of cash-all the things that would truly surprise me. I figured he'd gotten me some gummy worms or a coconut Yoo-hoo, both of which I loved. And before I could finish my thoughts, He walked in-Ron. WTF! What was he doing here? I wasn't expecting him. And...I had some other things going on. I'd been going to LIC practices regularly and had my eye on one of their new dancers, Jered. I know. I couldn't get enough of those dancers!

Jered was a medium glass of Nestle Quik chocolate milk that moved like Michael Jackson. His skin was smooth, his teeth were white, and his body was perfect. His ass was round and firm, and his abs were settled in 6 distinct squares. Packed! He knew that I was checking him out-catching my eyes as they followed him with every turn, squat and pelvic thrust. Again, I was in love. Eventually, we conversed, and he'd given me a couple of rides home, passionate kisses and fake orgasms. I never told him I had a boyfriend.

Trying to appear as normal as possible, I greeted Ron with a smile and a tight hug, all while looking at Kevin out of the corner of my eye. I wanted to strangle the shit out of him. Ms. Nichols included LIC in the upcoming recital and guess who was a part of the group? Yes. Jared. Ron was visiting for several days, so there was no way out of the shit show I'd created for myself. I couldn't miss practice, nor could I put Ron off on anyone, so I had to take him to practice with me. I was not excited about Ron's visit.

The first person I see, standing on stage, is Jared. And he saw me. He looked me straight on, in my eyes and I knew he noticed Ron. Ron didn't walk in after me or before me. We were shoulder to shoulder, so our "togetherness" was obvious. My face looked uneasy. Jared saw that too. I knew that he knew. My practice was fucked. I was fucked. Everything was fucked. I was not good at lying, so I knew this situation wouldn't end well. I was going to lose my Miami play-toy and my man.

As I'm moving through my Josephine Baker piece, I'm thinking... "Jered will be done with me. Why didn't I just tell him? I'm sure he has someone too. Everyone has someone when you meet them, no matter what they say. The "someone" could be the "Convenience Piece," the "It's Complicated" piece, or the "In Between" piece. Everybody got somebody." And then I heard her voice, "Ms. Charkes, you wanna do that again? Cause I don't know where your head is. I need you to get it together. You will not get on my stage looking like a retired Josephine Baker." Yep, Ms. Nichols was calling me out-as she should have. I wasn't present. I was moving up and down the stage, thinking about how to get out of the mess I'd made for myself. Embarrassed, I gathered the piece of my ass that was handed to me and did my part again.

Things usually got hectic close to recital time. Ms. Nichols' patience got short, her hand stayed on her hip and her right index finger remained in a pointed position. She wanted us to be as close to perfect as possible. I see the same with my sisters. They both are owners and artistic directors of dance studios and they put on at least two recitals a year (Exposure). And chile, when recital time draws near, they get to cussing and putting folks out. It's hilarious to watch, especially with my sister Simone. She cusses and says the funniest shit. "Girl, if you don't get your ass in the line, you gon be standing in line, at the front door, trying to get in the recital tomorrow." While the person in question is dying from embarrassment, everyone else is killing themselves trying not to laugh.

Practice was over and so were Jered and me. He walked up to me, asking who the guy was I'd walked into practice with, all while knowing exactly who he was. And of course, "Honest Abe" couldn't possibly tell a lie. She could've said…" Oh, that's my cousin." Or that's my bodyguard." Anything would have been better than, "that's my boyfriend." Jered looked at me like I was the worst person in the world and walked away.

Despite the demise of my love affair with Jered, I had to maintain the one I committed to. The one with Ron. So, I decided to make the most of his visit. It was summer, in Miami…so why waste it, right?

We decided on the Goombay Festival ("Goombay")-one of Miami's summer highlights at the time. The two-day festival, held in

Coconut Grove ("The Grove"), celebrated Bahamian culture as well as its contribution to American culture. As laborers, Bahamians were the first "Blacks" to settle in The Grove and they have maintained their physical and cultural presence in South Florida since. Who have you met that is a South Floridian, that doesn't have a Bahamian grandparent or parents? Hell, look at me. Also, Bahamians have significantly influenced South Florida dining. Outside of peas and rice, the "other white meat", conch, is a staple in many restaurants, diners and food trucks. Everybody loves conch salad. And nowadays, everybody (claims to) knows how to make it. You have your traditional, Bahamian style salad-containing fresh lime, conch, onion, sweet pepper, tomato, cucumber and hot peppers. Then you have tropical conch salad that includes whatever tropical fruit you choose. Usually pineapples. And then there's the "red" version where tomato juice is added to the traditional style ingredients. I prefer traditional conch salad. Not only is it the best, but Babalu would roll over in his grave at the thought of me partaking in any other version. Some things just need to be maintained in their original state. And conch salad is one of them. Along with Frankie Beverly's, "Before I Let Go". Ion know why Beyonce ain't leave that song alone.

Ron and I caught the Metro Rail to Goombay. It was, and still is, Miami's only rapid transit system. The Metro Rail stops at 23 stations, covering Miami International Airport to Dadeland Mall, including Coconut Grove.

While I don't remember what I wore, Ron's outfit was one that I'd never forget. Even twenty-four years later my brain's eye recalls his outfit. Having just pledged Omega Psi Phi, Ron was adorned in metallic gold combat boots, purple thigh-high shorts and a purple sleeveless t-shirt, that featured the symbol of his fraternity. You could also see the keloid branded Omega marks at the top of his arms, just below both his shoulders. He was sure to let everyone know he was a Que. He was proud to be a part of the organization and even more proud to openly represent it. I was proud of him as well.

Ron began pledging shortly after we started dating. Before attending Bethune Cookman, the only Greek organizations I'd been exposed to were the ones on the movie "School Daze". I was beyond ignorant. So, when Ron would get missing at night, my first thought was not pledging an organization. I was thinking his ass was pledging some girl. Cheating. My temperament was no different, then, than it is now. So, I imagine that I gave him hell about his whereabouts. He finally fessed up to what he was doing on the nights I couldn't find him. Well not totally. But I got the picture. Once his pledging process was complete, I swelled with pride. Not only was I, a freshman, dating the band's drum major but I was also dating an Omega Man! Every chance I got, with every penny I had, I'd run to the nearby paraphernalia store, "Just Off Campus" to buy Omega T-shirts for Ron. It was an exciting time for him, and I wanted to be a part of it as much as I could.

The pinnacle of Ron's outfit was his hair. Ron started out with six, thick cornrow braids, and by the time we left The Grove, he'd taken half of them down. Yep, Ron thought he was Method Man. While walking through the festival, I could see him unravelling them. Starting from the end, his thick middle and index fingers interrupted each crossing that made up a braid. As I watched, I mumbled to myself, "I know this muthahfuckah ain't taking out his braids." "Why Jesus? Why must he always do this? If he ain't walking the campus with his Johnson swinging because he refuses to wear drawz, he's excessively gyrating at the gym parties. Always making himself obvious. I was embarrassed. He was intentionally bringing attention to himself. I mean this type of behavior is fine for college in Daytona Beach, FL. But honey we were at the Goombay, where everyone from "The City" was hanging out that weekend. Everyone would be fly as hell in Daisey-Duke short sets, asymmetrical stacked weaves, sandals, white t-shirts, jean shorts and Jordan sneakers. Not hot ass gold work boots, male P.E. shorts and Ole Dirty Bastard hairdos.

All I could do was shake my head because there was nothing I could do or say to stop him. He enjoyed the attention.

Despite the spectacle, we managed to get through our outing without anyone recognizing me. So, the weekend was saved. For a moment. But then I thought, "Bitch, you told your family that you would come by the house today." Yeah, my day was not over. I had to take Method Man to the projects to Babalu and my siblings.

We got off at the Northside station and caught the "79" bus to 22nd Avenue and 79th Street. Once off the bus, we walked to my house, which was on 74th Street and 21st Avenue.

The residents of Scott Projects used their back doors as much as their front doors. Probably more. This was, in part, because the parking lots were in the back of the units. You'd frequently see people's back doors open, giving a full view of passersby. So, you know what Ron and I were about to embark on. As we walked, I ignored my peripheral vision. I wanted to act as if I didn't see people pointing, laughing and whispering. Ron didn't care, though. He was sure of himself. Well, at least he seemed to be.

In my wiser years, Ron's unconventional behavior is understood. Knowing him now, confirms his genuine individuality then. But I often wonder if part of what I and others experienced was insecurity-causing him to create another self-a layer of being formed to protect the parts of him he wasn't so sure of. Parts of him he wouldn't reveal because life had proved that they wouldn't be accepted. I'm sure you understand. I do. I've done it and still do, to a certain degree. I've always been a fragile little girl. Worried. Afraid. Never feeling safe. And even with that, life had requirements of me that forced an outer appearance of the opposite. Strong. Sure. Secure. The latter got praise, accolades and acknowledgement, while the former was never attended to. That hurt. Still does. In turn, I taught myself not to trust that part of me. I taught myself to be strong, and resilient. Let a niggah know that I don't need them. I can take care of myself and then some. But underneath, I scream for someone to save me. To stand by my side always ensuring safety. Letting me know that everything would be ok. No one ever listened, so I tucked that part of me away.

Ok, we got off the subject. Where was I? Oh, ok…Ron and I were walking through the projects, and I was shitlessly embarrassed, and he was acting like he didn't look crazy as hell. We finally reached my unit. I could see that Babalu and Chaz were already outside. They'd seen me approaching, so they remained put until we reached.

And then there we were. Standing and looking. I could tell Chaz wanted to ask Ron what the fuck was wrong with his head. But he didn't. For as long as I could remember, Chaz was polite. I introduced him, they shook hands and we turned towards Babalu. "Babalu, this is my boyfriend, Ron." He leaned in, and with closed eyes, he replied, "Who?" Which was his usual response. Most times it was because he didn't understand what was being said. You know, the American accent and all. He'd been in the United States for more than 30 years and still didn't fully understand American slang. But this time his "who" wasn't "please repeat that." His "who" was, "Who the fuck is this niggah?" (In a heavy Bahamian accent). I repeated his name, "Ron". "Oh, dis ya boyfriend, aye", he replied. I said, "Yes". He said, "Oh, ok", chuckled and went about his business. Babalu would usually have more to say, but knowing him, his chuckle said it all.

After visiting my family, we headed out to Sherrae and Kevin's. They were gone on vacation, so Ron and I had the place to ourselves.

Suddenly, I was overwhelmed with guilt. I felt the urge to tell Ron about my summer love affair with Jered. The entire trip back to Sherrae and Kevin's apartment, I'm thinking "Bitch, you gotta tell him." "You know you can't hold shit, so you may as well fess up to yo hoeish ways." Ron could tell I was distracted. But I offered "nothing" when he asked if I was ok.

We finally got to the apartment. Ron and I were sitting on the living room sectional, watching T.V. and suddenly my big ass mouth opened. "I've been cheating on you." I laugh as I write this because I had to be the biggest dummy in the world. Why on earth I admitted to seeing someone else, I don't know. Especially since Jered had dumped me days before at dance practice. So, Ron didn't have to know. There was dead silence. For at least 2 minutes, Ron didn't speak a word. I didn't know what to think. Was he going to choke my ass or cry like a baby? And then he got up and walked outside, through the parking lot of the apartment complex. I immediately went to the kitchen and got the biggest knife I could find. Shit, he hadn't said anything and was walking around like a zombie, so I had to prepare myself in case he had problems processing what I'd told him. I grabbed the knife and walked to a window where I could see him. He was walking in circles as if he was lost. I thought, "Bitch, you fucked up". "That's what your ass gets for trying to be a player." "Now you ain't got naauh one of them." "You a hoe in both of their eyes." Ron eventually disappeared from the parking lot. I assume he'd called his fraternity brother Russell to come and get him.

CHAPTER 4

INTERVIEWED ENTRY

The next school year had come and gone. I'd managed a g.p.a. of 3.5 and had selected nursing as a major. As a final determinant of "fit" for the program, all potential nursing students had to interview with division leadership. My interview was carried out by and with the Dean of Nursing, Dr. Biggs. She stood about 5'1", was bald and had beautiful, white teeth. She also had long nails. They were 3-inch acrylics, painted bright red. This was odd to me, as I wouldn't have thought someone of her caliber, a career woman, would wear long fake nails. I'd only seen similar nail lengths and colors worn by girls in the projects. While I realize she was far removed from the bedside, the standard, of what I thought was professional, should have been maintained.

Sitting behind a huge mahogany desk, Dr. Biggs greeted me, "Hello". She seemed comfortable and pleased that I was there. I greeted her back, saying the same. "Hello". She then asked that I tell her about myself and why I was choosing nursing as a career. Nervously, I responded. "My name is Charkes Nesbitt". "What an idiot you are", I thought. "She knows your damn name. It's sitting in front of her on your application." I went on and spoke about Miami, Liberty City and that I was the eldest of my mother and father's nine children. That was always the best icebreaker for me. People, including Dr. Biggs, were always amazed by my big family. And the fact that I am the eldest, is even more intriguing. I told Dr. Biggs that I chose nursing because it was a safe profession, and it would put me in a financial situation to help my family. I also added that I loved helping people. "Helping" is why most healthcare workers chose the field. At least back then it was. Nowadays, nursing is all about cash. Between the license fraud scandals and the financially lucrative travel assignments-helping is lost in art and intention in nursing.

But helping was natural for me. It was also intimate. From the time I could remember, I was caring for my siblings. I cooked for them, washed their clothes, did their hair and made sure they went to school. They were like my children. My life had already laid the foundation for what was to come in career. There was no other choice.

Dr. Biggs and I rambled on for about an hour. She spoke of her son and husband, both of whom she seemed to adore. We also talked about our hairstyles. They were similar.

Back then, I wore a boy's haircut- a bald fade. I had no hair from the mid-circumference of my head to the nape of my neck. The hair on the top of my head was faded into the bald area. I wore this hairstyle for more than a decade and loved it. It was low maintenance and made me feel bold and beautiful. Between band practice, performances and studying, I didn't have the time or money to maintain my hair. So, I cut it. The change was extreme. Most women adore their hair. It's a prime factor in beauty. For centuries we've added hair, through wigs or extensions, to be the "most beautiful girls in the world." So, my decision to cut mine-to shift from what is considered beautiful- was confusing for many. And still is. The other extremity in my choice in hairstyle was that I was a 14Kt. Gold Dancer. Never in the history of the group had any dancer worn their hair as short as mine. The idea was not heard of because it was never spoken. All 14Kt. Gold Dancers were expected to wear hair extensions. Weaves. Didn't matter the style, as long as the weave was long enough to accentuate your dance moves-according to our leader back then. Well, that was a bunch of hogwash to me. Anyone that has ever followed dance knows that professional women dancers have been bald, worn their hair in tight buns, and afros. Proving that hair doesn't make the dance. The dancer does. Needless to say, my new "do" didn't go over well with the team's captain. I remember the day like yesterday. We'd gathered in the band room for a spring performance. The room was filled with members and their chatter-as always was the case when everyone got together. I walked in and you could hear a pin drop. The captain looked at me with disdain. She couldn't believe her eyes. If she could cuss, and not get in trouble, she would have. And if she were light skinned, I'm sure I would have been able to count every vein in her forehead. That's how pissed she was. She looked at me and I looked at her. And she looked at me again, and I looked right back at her. There was an exchange in words in between the looks. She told me that I couldn't perform with such short hair. Not like that, but something to close. Chile please. From that moment on, hair never reached my ear. Her telling me what I couldn't do, made me do it. And my hair had nothing to do with my skill. Hair was not a membership requirement, and it certainly wasn't mandated for performance. It wasn't written. And if it aint written, it aint happening. "I am not my hair!" (In my India Arie voice).

I think Dr. Biggs saw a lot of herself in me. This reflection turned our interview into a conversation between kindred souls. And guess what? That connection lent to my acceptance into Bethune-Cookman College's School of Nursing. I was on my way.

Fun fact. My hair now is as bald as Dr. Biggs' was back then. And, I'm the nursing leader with 3-inch red acrylic nails! Lesson-"Keep Living".

For the last two years of college, I took Nursing classes all day, attended band practice in the evening and performed almost every weekend for 3 months (during the fall semesters). My schedule was taxing. It exhausted me-literally and figuratively. Nursing required heavy ass books and even heavier studying habits. I'm serious. I had a Medical-Surgical Nursing book that was at least 48 inches thick, almost twice as long and weighed about 5 pounds. I had to carry that book across campus, 3 times a week, in addition to at least 3 other books. We hadn't progressed to electronic textbooks yet, so all books were live, in color and in hand.

I used notes taken during class and extended them using an outline method. I also incorporated an audio means of studying by listening to free online presentations. The downside was that I had to listen to the presentation multiple times because my day's exhaustion would put me to sleep immediately. The presentations became lullabies instead of study guides.

Listening and learning helped with subjects like pathophysiology-which was extremely granular. The terms were unfamiliar, long and required phonetic pronunciation at times. Take atherosclerosis for instance. It is the hallmark process in coronary artery disease. I imagine these words being unfamiliar to most of you, especially the former. Now pronounce it. Yep, feel like you're in elementary school, huh? And once you finally get the terms down, you then must understand their processes. Yes. Processes. What is atherosclerosis and how does it lead to coronary artery disease? What is coronary artery disease? For those who are not medical practitioners, coronary artery disease is usually the condition that causes heart attacks. You know, when Fred Sanford told Elizabeth he was coming to see her because he was having "the big one". Yeah, that. Atherosclerosis is caused by inflammation, which creates the environment for plaque formation within the arteries that feed the myocardium (heart muscle). Multiple terms, and processes stacked on top of processes. All for me to get a job making $13.01 an hour. Chile please.

And once we had our footing in health and disease, we had to apply it as nurses. This is where the "Art of Nursing" comes into play. We were not physicians, nor would we be practicing as such. So, what on earth did we do with a patient who suffered from a heart attack? We created nursing diagnoses and care plans that aligned with the effects and manifestations of a heart attack:

Reduced oxygenated blood flow to the brain, heart, kidneys and lungs.

In turn, a nurse would diagnose this patient with Altered Tissue Perfusion. The corresponding plan of care would include, but not limited to:

1. Frequent Vital Sign Monitoring (blood pressure, heart rate, respirations, temperature, pain)

2. Urine Output Monitoring

3. Oxygen Saturation Monitoring

4. Cognition/Awareness Monitoring

This scheme applies to every disease state.

My nursing student life was demanding, but I loved every bit of it. I got high off extensive reading, detailed note taking, and last-minute cramming sessions. I enjoyed being able to dissect foreign concepts and apply them in my head, and then in real-life human disease states. I relished in the discipline of learning and the standards that were upheld for clinical rotations-all white uniforms, ironed crisp and stainless. The fact that our nails had to be natural and un-polished and that our earrings had to be almost invisible gave the profession meaning. Having to report to the hospital the evening before clinical to receive our patient assignment, understand their ailments, and the drugs they were prescribed, and have all the information organized and documented as Nursing Diagnoses was intoxicating. The chef's kiss was having to and successfully balancing band through it all.

I operated this way in college and once I graduated. Honestly, I can't think of a time when I didn't run my life this way. High school was the same. I was geographically zoned for The West but opted to attend a school more than 20 miles away from home. The West was, literally, a hop, skip and jump away from Scott Projects. I had quite a time in elementary and middle school with bullying and not belonging, so I decided to change my environment for secondary school. I chose to attend G. Holmes Braddock Sr. High (Braddock). I didn't know what was to come with Braddock, but it had to be better than the constant cackling and nit picking about the shoes I wore, how many wrist bangles I didn't have, how nappy my hair was or how my acid wash jeans looked "homemade". I was looking for Braddock to offer what Orchard Villa and Drew Middle didn't. And what The West wouldn't-inclusion and acceptance.

Because Braddock was so far away, I had to get up around 4:45am to catch my assigned bus at 5:30am. I was one of the first stops of the bus route-giving reason as to why I had to be up so early. The school bell rang at 7:15am and our asses had to be in first-period class seats at 7:30. But by the time I'd reached senior year, Robyne and I weren't getting up that early for school. We were going to the nearby park. If I were presented with a summary of my attendance for that school year, I'd be surprised if I were present half of the time. I honestly don't know what Robyne and I were thinking by going through all that trouble to get to school and not go. Our lack of engagement was clear but not because Braddock was bare in educational challenge. Both Robyne and I took advanced placement (AP) classes. Mine was Language Arts. In hindsight, we both had the same longings. Present parents. Love. And affirmation. While the latter was filled through each other, the former remained unattended to.

CHAPTER 5:

HURT

Writing brings me so much freedom. (Pause and refresh your thoughts-like sniffing coffee beans after testing perfume.)

I've been taken to a place of thought (again). A place I was not going until now. As I detail the business of my formative years, I'm pressed with thoughts about what I was doing while taking up every minute of that time with school and dance. I think about why I chose to wake up earlier and go to bed later. And why the time between rising and falling was so pervasive. I think about why I chose school and dance and not the streets and boys. These options were easier and readily available. But since I've known myself, I've made good decisions. It was expected of me. As a little girl, I was given adult responsibilities and accepted them as a woman would. Turns out, being a good decision maker meant that I was responsible and being responsible was the only way I was seen. It was the only positive con-sensus about Charkes' character that would get people to say, "good job" or "you're enough". It became my ego. My protector. It covered the parts of me that were un-attended to. The parts of me that were tender and easily hurt due to neglect. So, the more responsible I was, the more recognition I got. By the time I was school age, I was cook-ing, cleaning and tending to my brothers and sisters-by myself. And by the time I reached teenage years, I was a full-blown mom.

I imagine my ego telling my other self, my hurt self, "I know your parents never told you they loved you or that you were worthy of love, but at least other people say you're smart. And now, you're the boss. You take care of everyone. And they need you to. Just take that until you find someone to love you." And if you don't, I'll always be here for you to fall back on. Your brain and mother instincts are more important than your heart."

But there was another side to my "responsibleness"-being able to escape. School was the gateway to my freedom. It allowed me to break away from the responsibilities of caretaker. It was the only way I could. Babalu wouldn't argue it because going to school was the right thing to do. It was expected. So, when I got on the bus, Babalu knew I was doing what I was supposed to -going to school and engaging. He never inquired about what I learned or my grades. He never asked about plans after high school. He didn't believe he needed to. Not with me at least. I was the responsible one.

While my circumstance was more than ideal to most teenagers, it saddened me. It left me lonely-at home and in life. I longed for guidance. I yearned for parenting. I wished Babalu would've asked about the ins and outs of school, what my favorite subject was and what I wanted to study in college. I wish he would have asked for my report card, scolded me for poor grades and then told me how I could do better, cause I was better. He never did. Nobody ever did. I was the responsible one. I had no one to look up to. Only people who looked up to me. *(HURT)*

Even after graduating college, I continued the same behavior. I chose what "seemed" right, despite how flawed some of my decisions turned out to be. I made one decision after the next, never pausing to thinking about what life had done to me. Only later in life did I realize that my life had created a person that could stand tall despite horrid circumstances, while also fabricating a person that would perpetuate similar circumstances in life ahead. Basically, the driving force that caused success in education and career would be the same force that caused defeat in love, romance and career.

A year after completing studies at Cookman, I got pregnant, worked up until the end of my pregnancy, had Adrian, moved from Daytona (Florida) to Miami (Florida), from Miami to Melbourne (Florida) and then from Melbourne back to Daytona. And when Adrian turned

2, I started graduate school at The University of Florida (2 hours away from Daytona). I did this, all, while working full time as a float nurse at Halifax hospital, as adjunct faculty at Cookman, and as a nurse for Star-Med staffing agency. My ego was in full gear. I was doing everything right. Except pausing. I was moving while hurt; and work, school, and now, mothering, were my ways of coping-even when I didn't realize it. Hurt had been growing in my belly since childhood, and with Adrian, I was double pregnant. He was my only birth though. My other baby stayed and remained with me-even as I finish this paragraph.

My life was void of basic love and filled with abuse. And here I was beginning a life with a man and bearing his child but couldn't define love and family healthily. The folks that were supposed to exemplify healthy love were either beating the shit out of the person they said they loved or beating the shit out of me cause their lover didn't love them the way they needed to be. And I'd be remiss if I didn't mention the fondling of my private parts when I was a little girl, by folk that were supposed to protect me. So, what did I know about love? What did I have to offer this man and his unborn son? I was repeating life as I'd experienced it as a child. And no matter how mature and maternally experienced I thought I was, I was not prepared to be a wife or a mother. My ego was about to be in the fight of its life.

My relationship with Adrian's dad was the first to reveal the hurt I was carrying. The hurt due to not receiving basic love. I jonesed for it. Love was my achilles heel and then it made me an achilles heel. It made me weak and caused blind spots to standards that should have been established and upheld as boundaries. I conceded in ways I shouldn't have. Because of love's pull, I didn't take time to get to know him before parentally committing to him. I was pregnant after three months of courtship and I allowed him to control me with jealousy and isolation. I thought he was loving me. My hankering for deep affection overshadowed rationale. It fought my ego for top spot in my head and heart and won every time.

But I kept moving. Despite love's predicament, I managed to propel myself through finish lines one would consider extraordinary. I'd earned the degrees, made the money, and became "THE PERSON". But I still felt despondent. I didn't have anyone to look up to. There wasn't a person that would nod my approval or mouth, "I love you". The people that should have done so were only figures of my imagination. My mother had long been homeless, and my father was out of site and mind.

In motion, I constantly looked around for help. A helpmate. Someone to help with the pain I carried with me daily-for years. During one of our many arguments, I remember telling my ex-husband that I needed him to carry some of my pain-so I didn't feel alone. The selfishness of emotion made that request seem sensible. But the ask was incomprehensible because it wasn't his responsibility to carry my pain. He had his own. He was hurt too. But emotion only feels what it feels and causes the person experiencing it to feel isolated. And there's no way two emotionally isolate people can come together as one. They both show up hurt and lack vulnerability but want their partner to un-guard and repair situations they had nothing to do with. My father criticized me heavily so when my partner disapproves of a character trait, I don't hear my partner, I hear my father. At which point, I'm hurt. Not solely hurt from my partner's comments but taken back to the last time my father criticized me and then respond from that place. Meanwhile my partner is being triggered by my response to his disapproval. This cycle of events continues until one or both partners acknowledge the pattern, recognize their hurt space(s) and why, and does the work to move forward in a healthier relationship. Otherwise, demise is inevitable.

And then someone finally comes along who seems to want to join me. I think, "maybe with company, I'll feel better and stop constantly moving. In the beginning, I'd be hopeful. I'd tell myself, "It's finally my time to have the partner I've been dreaming of all my life." Someone who will not only move with me but also make sure I take water breaks and ask me if I'm good as I stride. Someone to say, "take a break", because they know me well enough to know that I will keep going despite fatigue. They know me well enough to know what drives the constant motion. They would rub my ugly ass feet during rest and not refuse because "they don't do feet".

But he eventually finds me unattractive and moves on. Not physically or sexually but temperamentally. By this time, my ego has been beaten by the urgency to be loved. It shows up differently. It shows up anxiously. It shows up in the past while standing dead in the present.

After Ron, there was Haze. He was a light skinned bowlegged brother from New York that loved basketball and DMX. He had an old soul that was also non-trusting. If he called and I didn't answer right away, he'd query me about my whereabouts when he called. He'd probe with multiple questions toned as if he were my pimp disrespecting him by not being readily available. He'd even pop up at me and Alice's apartment late at night and would get mad because I didn't hear his call or knock at the door. He never formally decided that I was his girlfriend, but he expected me to behave like I was.

Then there was Adrian's father. I'll leave him nameless, cause he doesn't deserve that degree of acknowledgement. But I must detail our relationship because he contributed to my journey-significantly. He's my son's father.

We met at the gym. My friend Cicely and I were getting our fine on, I saw him looking and told Cicely to give him my number. He was good-looking, tall, and medium-built. I remember the first time we had sex. Immediately afterwards, he asked, "What does this mean?" And my dumb ass answers, "we together". I won't say my relationship with him was a mistake, cause I love my son. He is the best thing about my life. But his daddy. Chile, please. I'd say about 3 months into our relationship I was pregnant. Yep. And it was during my pregnancy I found out he was still living with his first baby-momma. And-she and I worked at the same hospital. I discovered this when I went to take a patient's belongings to the accounting office. That's what we did back then to secure personal items until discharge from the hospital-complete an itemized document, drop items into a clear bag, along with a copy of the document, seal the bag and deliver it to accounting for safe keeping.

On the day at hand, I see a young lady with a ring on her left ring finger. Not sure why I noticed it first. Maybe because I've always been so thirsty to get married that I always surveyed people in my immediate space to see who was married. I would compare the single folk to myself with the hopes of feeling better about not being married.

I looked at her name badge. Then I look at her face and recall the conversations I'd had with him, about her. Then I think, well I'll be damned". This is her. Why didn't he tell me that she works here? And I thought they had broken up? Why is she wearing a ring? I confronted him about what I saw, and of course, he didn't have much to offer in terms of reasoning. He never left her alone. He was still formally living with her while laying his big ass head at his mom's house and in my bed. I assume she got word of who I was and our pregnancy. And from that point on, she caused pure hell in my life. Now, I understand why. But when I was in her hell, I did not.

She spread rumors, at the hospital, about the father of my child-claiming that I'd been involved with a young man who worked in the laundry department. She even told him the same and he believed her. This triangular drama continued even after he finally left their relationship. While in labor with Adrian, he had to attend child support court for their children. And although he made it back in time, the fate of our relationship was set at that point. We were misaligned. He hadn't finished business with her before he'd gotten into a relationship with me and I obviously hadn't checked to see if his business was finished before I committed to him.

They'd had a baby three months before we met, which I didn't know until a month into our courtship. He didn't have a place of his own which meant he'd always have to be at my place (that I shared with Alice), or we'd have to hang out at his mother's house. He'd proven that he wasn't ready to start a new family and didn't have the means to support theirs or ours. So, why did you continue a relationship with him? Was it because healthy relationships weren't exampled for me? Was it because I didn't regard what was necessary to maintain a relationship as important; engaging with a person that was single, self-sufficient, and secure? Was it because I hadn't acknowledged those things within myself, holding them as standards instead of options? Or was it because I'd grown used to accepting what I knew wasn't right? Always receiving people wherever they are and despite their inability to serve and provide for me, telling myself, "I'll be alright"?

It's a sequela. The initial injury-abandonment. The consequential condition-self abandonment. *(HURT)*

I remember writing a paper in undergraduate school about the psychosocial effects of single parenting on adolescent children. I wanted a better understanding of the immediate and long-term effects of being brought up by one parent. Did adolescents require more guidance and supervision at this age? Did they need more emotional support? And if they didn't get it, what did it lead to? Jail? More single parenting? Substance abuse? While I don't remember the conclusion I came to, something is overwhelmingly apparent to me now: I should have written a paper on the psychosocial effects of burdening elderly children with adult responsibilities. What happens when a child is forced into parenting, and homemaking too early- even before their own reproductive organs and minds have developed enough to handle such responsibilities? I say this premature exposure fosters excessive understanding, making it difficult for the child to create and maintain boundaries in adulthood, including boundaries with the children/siblings they helped raise. Premature exposure to adulthood also gives the adult child a false sense of assurance and grandiosity, which makes them feel more important than they are. These children eventually have problems with leadership and authority because they have always been the authoritative figure. They made the decisions. They managed the house. They guided the children/ siblings. And more importantly, these adult children miss out on important stages of psychosocial development, causing personality deficits. In essence, they mis-develop. Erik Erikson's psychosocial stages of development theory explain it best- "Social experiences are valuable throughout life, and to be fully functional members of society, we must successfully complete each stage and resolve two conflicting states. For example, stage 4 of this theory notes that education and socializing are inherent to healthy psychosocial development at ages 5-12 years old. Successful learning and peer interactions are integral to their sense of competence. And failure results in feelings of inferiority. If a child is given parental responsibilities, at this age, they are at risk of missing school, either through tardiness or absenteeism. Maybe they've stayed up late getting their siblings ready for school the next day. Or, in my case, up at 3am doing laundry. In turn, the child is too tired to engage in school and too busy at home to complete homework. Then the child falls behind and inferiority kicks in. Yes, the child knows how to iron, cook, clean and do laundry, but these tasks don't lend to reading, writing or arithmetic-unless the child is intellectually exceptional-naturally. If so, they are at risk of failing socially by not interacting with or developing healthy relationships with peers. **(HURT)**

My relationship with Adrian's dad eventually came to a head. We engaged to be married, and then I left. I'd grown to know him as insecure, which showed up as controlling. His lack of trust showed up in the same way. I'd grown tired of the countless questions about being in relationships with men I hadn't spent 10 seconds of my day thinking about. Which is hypocritical, considering the situation he was in when we met. I guess that's why he didn't trust me. He didn't trust himself and what I'd experienced was pure mental projection. *(HURT)*

After Adrian's dad, there was a string of relationships I had no business in.

There was Will. He was married but separated. I knew this but acted like I didn't. Our conversations were filled with promises of divorce and happily-ever-afters.

I was excited when I got word that his house was being sold. That meant to me, that his divorce was finally on the way. To confirm what I'd heard, I did a drive-by like Monica and Missy. Sans the "kick down yah door and smack yah chick". I pull up, see his son outside and ask him to get his dad for me. He recognized me from a time we'd spent together, so he didn't have an issue with carrying out my request. Then out comes Will. He crossed the threshold of his front door and stepped onto his front porch. Once he recognized my truck and confirmed it was me that had pulled up to his house, unannounced, he looked to be to be having a silent stroke. He likely was in disbelief about my actions and was scared shitless about what was to come. As he walked down the steps, away from the front door, his wife appears. He looked at me, I looked at him, and she looked at me. Like a scene from an R. Kelly video. Will walked over to my car, stuck his head in the passenger window and relaxed his arms on the door. "What's up", he asked. I went on to ask him why he hadn't told me that he sold his house. All while Mrs. Will is asking who I was. Like Lorraine was in "What's Love Got to Do with It". "Who is she, Ike"? "Who is she, Will"?

I laugh now, but the situation was not comical. Me rolling up to a married woman's house to see why her husband hadn't disclosed a house sale that I had no ownership in was downright stupid. I was non-sensible and immature. I was hankering for love. My desire for the man and the relationship was more important than respect for a woman and her family. It was more important than respect for my-self- I showed my dumb ass up at someone's house to confirm what I already knew. My desire was more important than respect for their kids. I got his son involved and had him bear witness to an unhealthy relationship *(HURT)*. We ended up in an O.J. Simpson-type situation. I drove off, Will followed me and Mrs. Will followed him. She eventually grew tired of the slow-speed chase and veered off in the opposite direction. As did me and Will's relationship.

I mean, what was I expecting? For him to leave his wife and children, right out? Right away for me? I was too green to understand the dynamics of marriage and too thirsty for love and relationship to walk away when I learned he was married. The way I was carrying myself and behaving was a mirror image of the dysfunction I saw in my parents' relationship. It was what I saw my dad do to my mother. It was what I witnessed with my dad's "other" women who did not care about my mother or the 8 children she bore for my dad. Nor did they care that he lied in bed with her after their sex-filled ran-devu. Those women's desire for my dad outweighed the extensions of him that would fall victim to their selfish love affair. They wanted him more than they wanted peace. They wanted him more than they wanted themselves. And I was no different.

There I was, again, pouring into a relationship that would never provide a refill. There I was again, **HURT.**

After Will, I found a distant lover. I decided to get closer and moved. Again "married but separated". I'm shaking my damn head about this as I am reminded of the mistakes I made repeatedly.

I met this guy by the way of a trip I'd taken, with someone I knew. We talked and connected through art. He was an up-and-coming movie producer who I found never really produced anything except a home movie that starred his brother, cousins and cousins-in-law years before we'd met.

There I was again, listening to a separated married man talk about his wife and how unhappy he was in their relationship. And again, the desire to BE WITH outweighed the desire to BE WITHOUT!

I listened long enough to quit my job and move me and Adrian's black asses across state lines. Only to arrive and be ready to go immediately. I had to take out a personal line of credit from One Main Financial to cover the moving expenses. Yep. You read that right. The negro couldn't even help me move. I had to rent the moving truck and put the money down on the place we were supposed to move in.

So, check it out, we get to our new place and the people hadn't even finished cleaning it. The carpet was filthy, which was, and still is, a no-no for me. I like to LIVE in my home. That includes walking barefoot on, and even sleeping on the carpet. I couldn't be comfortable with all the doo-doo, cat dander, dog hair, street gum and pee that was transferred from someone's shoe, finding its final resting place within the fibers of my pile. I was overwhelmed with disappointment and regret. How did I get myself in such a situation? I had a great job, apartment and life. Yet, I chose to leave all of that behind for a state and man I knew nothing about. This wouldn't be my first time in this predicament.

I immediately asked the owners for my deposit back and went on to search for somewhere else to live.

We finally landed in a 3-bedroom apartment.

He never divorced. And although we were getting ready to live together, he still lived with his wife (by the time I'd moved, he was living in the basement). Sound familiar? Being in between houses, which included two school-aged children, he couldn't afford to support Adrian and me the way he was supposed to. All bills were split down the middle and only my salary afforded us a decent quality of life. He went along on the ride but knew he was in over his head. And so was I. His wife found out about me and our living situation and made his life a living hell. He would complain about it and her, constantly calling her "Bitch" as he grieved. And his children got on my nerves. It was no fault of theirs. I was used to one child and wasn't ready for additional parental responsibilities-especially for kids that weren't raised with the standards I'd established with Adrian:

Answer "Yes" when adults call you or speak to you.

Take your shoes off in the house.

Verbalize your thoughts and quit nodding your damn head and shrugging your shoulders when you are spoken to!

Don't come to me with all that damn crying and whining. Figure it out.

You eat what's cooked or you starve until the next meal.

And bedtime is at 9 o'clock, not when you feel like it.

The end of our relationship came when I purchased a house in a nearby city. Notice the "I" and not "we". I'd finally closed and was preparing to move in. And, no, he didn't provide a down payment, closing costs or a love offering. He only offered his frugality. We'd visited American Signature Furniture to look for and purchase a new bedroom set. Now why I set myself up for disappointment, I don't know. He'd already established that he was cheap and was okay sleeping anywhere flat while being itched to death by 200 thread count sheets containing cotton boogers. We oscillated about the cost of the bed set-mattress, box spring, headboard, and footboard. He swore he could get the same quality cheaper-somewhere else. "Man, ain't nobody paying that much for no bedroom set. You can go over to Badcock and get the same thing for less." I ignored him with the deepest ignoration I could find. Cause I was getting the bedroom set I wanted.

We moved in, and soon after, the mattress and box spring arrived. The delivery team set them both upstairs in the master bedroom. The remaining pieces wouldn't be delivered for several days. That night, I retired early. I was exhausted from the constant back and forth from the moving truck to the house. And I wore myself out even more because I moved everything in one day. I hear the garage door open and his car driving in. So, I turned over on my left side, in bed, and played possum. I was over him. I didn't want to be near him, nor did I want him in my house or in my bed.

Once upstairs, the negro undressed, lied down on the mattress and almost had an orgasm because of how comfortable it was. "God-damn, this mattress is comfortable. Damn. Oooh. Ahh." I couldn't believe it. I thought, "This couldn't be the same man who wanted a rent-a-bed". No way possible was this the man that argued with me about paying, what he thought was, a fortune for a bedroom set. At that point, even more disgust, regret and resentment settled. The next day, I broke up with him and told him he had to leave my house immediately.

He left with his clothes, cotton booger sheets and ironing board mattress.

Then there was Sauken. I met him through a friend of a friend. We seemed to be more aligned. He'd gone to and completed college, had a career, and had a place of his own. He was extraordinarily handsome and had a sense of style that I appreciate as a grown(er) woman.

Sauken and I had quite a few interesting commonalities. His maternal grandparents' surname was Nesbitt. He'd hidden this from me until I'd gotten a chance to meet them. Sauken loved a "wow" factor and his ability to keep a secret. So, to see my expression upon revealing what he'd been holding for months made him profoundly happy. Sauken also shared my son's name. His middle name was Adrian. I became aware of this long before I learned his grandparents' name. This was a harder secret to keep because, "What's your middle name?", is a necessary and ice-breaking question at the beginning of relationships. He loved Adrian. He treated him like his own. We lived together, ate together and traveled together-as a family.

I loved Sauken's family as well. They accepted both my son and I as if I was his wife and Adrian came from both our loins. Everything was perfect. Until it wasn't. We argued-constantly. And every time we argued, I broke up with him. I was hurt from childhood, and my failed relationships. And this is where and how I showed up. What Sauken experienced each time I left was me protecting myself from further hurt. My ego-the strongest part of me- constantly fought love for first place in my head and heart. And by the time I'd met Sauken, ego was wining. The disagreements were about the simplest of things, but the crux was about what we needed from each other. He needed me to listen to him to feel respected as a man, which translated as control to me. I'd already lived a life under the thumb of my dad, who was the same person that gave me the autonomy of a fully grown adult. So, the requirement to "listen" triggered me for a myriad of reasons. Listening to Sauken meant that I had to allow him make decisions for me that I'd already made or could make for myself. Listening to him meant I had to follow his plan and position as instructed. I didn't need a mentor, father or dictator. I needed a partner. A man that would support me as I figured life out just as he was. Not someone looking to push me in a direction that was made for him, by him. My way of being was challenging for some men to relate to. My character fell out of the order of operations for women. I was more "man-like" than "woman-like". My character was too much for Sauken.

Sauken also needed a child of his own. Adrian wasn't enough. While he loved him, Adrian wasn't his child. He didn't bare his surname, have his hands, feet or eyes. He was another man's child. Two years prior to meeting him, I had a partial hysterectomy-making me permanently sterile. At the beginning of our relationship, I shared this with Sauken. And although he was verbally accepting of my situation, I felt as if he silently resented me for it. I know this is one of the other reasons we fought. I know that's why we couldn't live out our lives together. I was not able to confirm him as a man through behavior or creation. Hence, I had nothing to offer Sauken.

My relationship with him is one I often wonder about. *(HURT)*

After Sauken, my roster was plentiful, but without major plays. The men were self-centered, traumatized and controlling. And I was raw with hurt, while pretending to have it all together. The core of me had yet to be healed and ego was front and center. Protecting me. My initial engagements would start strong but end disastrously. And I ended up more hurt and alone.

One of the relationships had me so low that I thought of suicide. Often. This guy was angry. He was rage-filled and relentless when it was released. I remember an instance where he told the mother of his son that he wished he hadn't wasted his cum (semen) in her. I also remember the time he cursed me out, calling me a "Bitch" at one of his family gatherings, in front of his family. Elders and all. He'd interpreted my conversation with his cousin as disrespect. He kicked me out of the house and threw my keys at me as I walked to my car. And the time I had to put him out of my car, on I-85 N, during rush hour traffic was another bitch calling session.

I eventually discovered that his anger was passed down-like eye color and complexion, from a parent to a child. His anger was passed along by his father. As a boy, his father managed him by physically and mentally abusing him. He described a time when his dad picked him up and threw him across the room-in response to what one would consider "normal" school-aged boy behavior. He was an adult but stuck in the place he was last hurt. Stuck where his father first physically struck him. Stuck where the father-son bond was forever broken. Stuck where the suffering began, which was expressed through reckless and self-sabotaging behavior. He would drink until obtunded and drive like a criminal on a high-speed chase. He smoked more marijuana than the D O Double G, himself, and would always carry offendable amounts of it in his car. I was right there with all of it; right beside him expressing my "stuck".

The abuse from his dad was proof, to him, that he wasn't accepted. He wasn't good enough. This was an early recognition for me, so I tried to help. My ego was reporting for duty. But no matter what I did, how I soothed or supported him, one hint of challenge reminded him of insults from his father. If I commented on how much he smoked, he was triggered, and then I became the victim of the rage he felt for his dad. If I sought to make him accountable for his actions, he was triggered. He'd respond by criticizing me in the worse way- by bringing up something I shared with him during our up times. "You shouldn't have anything to say to me, you can't keep a man." Or he'd respond with a flat-out insult, "Fuck you Bitch.".

There I was carrying out the mis-development of my formative years. Remember what I said earlier about how obligations placed on adult children, as children, manifest in unhealthy ways when the adult children become adults? Well, this is an explicit example. My response here reveals how my childhood caused me to misunderstand understanding. My responsibility for my siblings required me to receive them without regard to temperaments. Even the conflicting ones. I had to be there for them without regard for myself, creating a capacity for people that would and has proved to be faulty. I was overly accepting, making boundary creation and maintenance challenging for me. Had I been allowed healthy mental and social development, I would have left his angry ass high and dry with the first whisper of the word "Bitch", or even when he cursed his Baby Momma out. I'll also add that growing up in the inner-city, men disrespecting women was commonplace. So, I felt right at home being verbally and emotionally abused. *(HURT)*

The other part of childhood conditioning that caused me to remain in such a relationship was mothering. I'd done it so early in my life and for so long, that I thought I could love everything away for him. I know I responded this way in all my romantic relationships. The men would say so in mentioning what they liked or loved about me. "You're nurturing." "I know you will take care of me." "You remind me of my mother." While those traits seem complimentary, they weren't. I'd developed them improperly, and therefore, they were placed improperly. I hindsight, my mothering skills weren't even effective with my siblings. I didn't possess the skills. I hadn't been parented and neither had I experienced life as I know it now. So, what was I providing them? My siblings needed more than me. They needed their own parents to love and guide them. They needed the people that made them to make them-better.

CHAPTER 6

EXITED-BARELY

graduated from Cookman in the summer of 1998. I couldn't walk with my class that spring because I'd failed a major exam. Bethune Cookman believes students "Enter to Learn and Depart to Serve". And while entrance was relatively easy, departure was more than challenging. In addition to standard coursework and corresponding exams, each department required potential graduates to complete and pass an exit exam. I failed the mine.

Before I dramatically depict that experience, I must let you know that I had one of the highest grade point averages in my class, wrote the best notes (which most in my class depended on), and was the recipient of a healthcare award in my senior year. Now-how and why in the hell did I fail the exam?

On a brisk Saturday, fall morning, we paraded to the campus library. Instructions were to report to the fourth floor, no later than 0800, with pencil in hand and a light sweater. (Who knew there was a 4th floor to the library I'd frequented for over 3 years). I was met with a thick musky smell of old books, wood and carpet. The room was dimly lit and far from cool. So, off came my light sweater. Scantron sheets were already placed on the tables we would sit at, and to the right, laid a dense book, titled "EPIC Nursing-An Exam". "What the hell is this", I thought. This exam book looked like nothing I'd seen during my time in the Nursing program. So, where did they get this? Would it be like the multiple exams I'd taken in our small classrooms that and reflective of the coursework we learned during the nursing program? I was more than nervous.

We were instructed to take a seat and get ready to begin testing. Once seated, we were given the rules of the road:

1. Take your time.

2. Think before selecting answers.

3. Don't overthink answers.

4. Don't look at anyone's answer sheet but your own!

5. Raise your hand if you need to take a break.

I opened the testing booklet and shuffled through its pages to see how many questions there were. 400. Immediately, my heart began to race. I felt it in my chest, and ears. I panicked. I knew it would take me forever to complete the exam-not because I wasn't knowledge-able, but because the exam appeared different. It wasn't the 1.5-2 pages we'd get on an early Friday morning, containing 40-50 questions. It wasn't created by instructors I'd sat with before, consuming their teaching style, cues, and subject knowledge. It was different, causing me to overthink questions and corresponding answers, and doubt myself. I knew I would fail.

About a week later, we got our exam results. Feeling queasy, I quietly leaned on the hallway wall- thinking about the 5 long hours it took me to answer all 400 questions, while listening to some of my peers scream in excitement about passing. I also watched others walk away with their heads tucked in disappointment because they hadn't. I finally gathered the courage to meet my fate. And as I knew, I'd failed. Emotionally distraught, I folded the exam document into my pocket along with my head. I was not only disappointed because I'd failed but also because some of the people who passed received a significant amount of help from me-throughout the program. I'd helped with concept explanations, note sharing, and study groups. How did they pass, and I hadn't? I was deeply upset.

Because so many of the failing students had concerns about the exam and its content, we grieved. And in turn, we were offered the opportunity to submit a formal grievance to the Dean of Education. I took full advantage.

I laid it all on the altar, telling the Dean about the testing environment, the type of test, the number of questions and how I didn't feel our coursework or curriculum aligned with the exit exam. She listened-sternly. She didn't crack a smile or offer any degree of comfort. She provided the facts of the exam-where it came from, why Cookman decided to use it and its contents. She, then, offered wisdom about accountability- "Accountability breeds responsibility". I got quiet. I looked her in her eyes, thanked her for the opportunity to discuss my concerns and embarrassingly exited her office.

The Dean was right, though. I needed to accept what happened as well as my responsibility in the failure and move forward with a plan to resolve and improve. I also had to accept the fact that there were some who passed the exam—nullifying my grievances.

To date, I hold accountability as an important character trait. Probably one of the most important. It's a constant point of conversation with my son. Failure to have this degree of personal insight causes developmental retardation. Without accountability, blame is always shifted and one never truly understands or accepts responsibility for their own lives, causing the experience of "stuck".

Concerning the exit exam, my responsibility was to trust what I knew and learned in the preceding years. Not doing so caused me to fail even before penciling my first answer.

I attended summer school, re-took the exam and passed. I graduated from Bethune-Cookman College in the summer of 1998, with a Bachelor of Science degree in Registered Nursing.

CHAPTER 7:

PERSONALITY AND CIRCUMSTANCE

The summer before graduation, I'd been living with the pastor and his wife. Both Alice and I were living with them. I'd met him during my freshman year. He was my Bible teacher. One day, during class, he asked if anyone wanted to make a couple of dollars. So, you know my hand was raised quickly and high. I was so naïve; he could have been asking me to scoop shit, and there I was auctioning myself off for God knows what, for a couple of dollars. But I needed the money. I couldn't ask Babalu for it and Sherrae and Kevin didn't have it to give constantly.

The pastor was newly married, his wife was pregnant, and they were moving from a nearby duplex to the parsonage. He needed someone to clean their duplex as they prepared for the move.

I got the job and the following weekend, I reported to work. The duplex had two bedrooms, 1 bathroom, a living room, a dining nook and a kitchen. A piece of cake for me. By then, I was a subject matter expert in cleaning. I'd spent a great deal of time cleaning behind 7 children, in homes twice the size of the pastor's dwelling.

I started with the bathroom. It proved to be the most tedious to clean, so it required most of my energy. They had a sliding door that sat on top of the tub. Something I had not seen until then. None of the tubs I'd bathed or showered in had a sliding door or even a shower curtain. Hell, you just put a towel on the floor and aimed the shower away from it, avoiding a tsunami once you finished. As I was cleaning the tub, I noticed this grey-looking substance that had accumulated in the bottom grooves of the door. You know the space where the doors slide and sit. I moved a little closer to better identify the substance before I touched it. And no, I ain't have no gloves. Despite damn there having my nose in the grey goo, I still didn't know what it was. And at that point, I was about to vomit. I was like, "What the fuck is that?" I took a deep breath, cringed my nose (like I am now) and scooped it up with the cloth I was using. I didn't get it all. So, I scooped again. "Whew", I thought. "That wasn't so bad." Until I slid the damn door to the other side where there was even more goo. I was ready to abort the mission, but continued to scoop until the grooves were free of the unidentified substance. Turns out, the goo was only soap scum. But how in the hell was I supposed to know?!

I eventually forged a lasting relationship with the pastor and his wife. I became the housekeeper even when they moved into the parsonage, and eventually, their babysitter. His wife-forever my second "God Sent" mother, and their daughter, forever my "God Sent" sister.

Life happens the way it's supposed to.

Alice's dad bought her a car for graduation—a hot pink Toyota Tercel. Odd color for a car, but a much-needed gift for both of us. Alice got to drive around the city as she pleased, and I got to ride shotgun. She also taught me to drive. Yes, I'd reached adulthood and didn't know how to drive. I didn't take driver's Ed. in high school and my only lesson was when my cousin Ken let me drive his car around in the back of Miami Dade Community College. I nearly drove into the nearby pond. I was immediately expelled from his driving course.

My brother Keo had a car though. Our dad bought him a one when he was 15. Mind you, Keo and I are exactly 10 months apart. I was born in January, and he was born in November of the same year. I was the most responsible of the two of us and was danm there an emancipated minor. But Babalu thought it was more important for Keo to have a car. That's how our dad was with his kids and his relationships. He held strong to his cultural, and gender positions and associated expectations. Women were secondary to men, and had primary responsibility in caretaking, and homemaking, while men were left to do as they pleased. I was in a patriarchy and didn't know it. I even carried some of these beliefs with me in adulthood. I always thought my responsibilities in romantic relationships were to generously sex, cook, clean and serve food to niggahs that weren't even my husband. Only to not be chosen in the end.

I was responsible enough to perform as an adult, but not enough to have a car? I believe Babalu's contrasted gendered treatment towards us molded our character, to some degree. To date, my brother Keo has a righteous heir about himself. My dad treated him that way. He got all the brags of being a good child by just being. He did keep a job and stayed out of trouble, but that didn't compare to the boulders I carried. And I managed to stay weed, baby, jail and disease-less while under his roof. But there wasn't a whisper of acknowledgment. Just more responsibility for being responsible.

As an adult, I am treated the same way. I receive very little acknowledgement for what I have done for my family, yet, continued matriarchal support is expected. Or maybe I continue to serve in that role without request or need. It confuses me at times. I'd call it a type of role confusion. I expect the praise of a mother from my brothers and sisters, and when I don't get it, I act out. Either in victimhood, singing "Woe is me" or by shutting down and isolating myself, which leads to depression. My siblings would then be confused because my response was bigger than the insult. In addition, I am their sister; their "Big Sister", but still, only their sister. My parents introducing me to them as a parent was improper and would prove to be a disservice to them and me in years to come. You've learned quite a bit about those disservices in this book. In addition, our family's parental-child mis-fit gave my siblings a sense of protection that would be short lived. My protection stopped where their hurt began. Hurt they couldn't share with me because, innately, they knew I didn't have the tools necessary to help them through. Hurt they wouldn't share because they naturally wanted and needed a, "Imma tell my momma" moment. I couldn't ease their pain because I was navigating my own hurt. Further proving they needed more than me and I needed more than them.

There was also a distinct difference in the way Babalu treated our brother Duke. By age 13, Duke was determined a menace to society. I remember him being featured in the article of the local newspaper, The Miami Times. The writer depicted Duke as a young sociopath, whose life trajectory was clear-death or jail. He went into detail about all the crimes Duke had committed by then and that he was finally sent to a detention ranch for troubled youth. The tone of the article was that of exasperation and hopelessness–like he was tired of young boys, like my brother, ending up in the system without hope for the future and not knowing what to do about it. By his early teens, Duke had robbed Zayre's, multiple jewelry stores, and carried out numerous snatch and grabs. He'd also admitted to being introduced to cocaine when he was 14 and had been chasing that high ever since. Considering such challenges, you'd think Babalu would focus on his needs, like he did Keo's. Instead, he focused more on the boy child who required less and whose character was more aligned with what was correct. There were even times when Babalu would instruct Keo to catch Duke after running from the police. Keo would get in his car and run him down like he was the police himself. Unbeknownst to Keo and the rest of us, our father was fostering divisiveness amongst his children.

Babalu, in some ways, created Duke's predicament by the communities we lived in. Settling in Liberty City exposed us to perilous situations, making Duke vulnerable to his environment. I'm sure you're asking, "what's the difference between him, you and Keo?" He could have made the decisions you all made. Some may easily say–" Do what Keo did." "Do what Charkes did." I wish it were that easy. Hell, I think Duke wished it were that easy. The truth is that Duke's personality caused him to respond to our circumstances in a negative way. While Keo and I did not require guidance to "do what was right", Duke did. He wasn't as self-directed and disciplined as Keo and I were. He required coaching and close guidance. He needed to be watered, fertilized, weeded and talked to. While Keo and I did that for ourselves. I've found myself saying and believing that a child's trajectory is not solely determined by his circumstances, but his response to those circumstances. And that response has all to do with personality. Circumstance + Personality=Outcome.

Not much has changed with Keo, Duke, or me. Keo and I remain outwardly successful, driven by our own desires. Meanwhile, Duke served 17 years in prison, after receiving two life sentences. He'd been released but re-offended and remains incarcerated. I've remained distant. My heart can't bear the burden of connecting anymore. Doing so takes both of us to places where we were last hurt. At which point, he'd be looking for me to mother him, and I'd easily settle into those expectations.

CHAPTER 8:

LIFE AFTER

Alice and I found a 2/1 in a nearby city. We were so excited! We both had jobs by then and managed to come up with enough money to buy two used bedroom sets and a used sofa- paired with a coffee table and two end tables. The sofa was likely from the 70's. It was made of a medium brown velvet fabric, with perfectly spaced pine trees all over. The only thing missing was the overlay of plastic everyone's grandma used to protect her "good furniture". Let me not forget the exposed piece of metal at the top right corner of the sofa. We had to warn everyone as they casually brushed along its right side, preventing injury from a cut.

I was working at Indigo Manor Nursing Home as a certified nursing assistant (CNA). Although I wasn't licensed as such, my nursing degree grandfathered me into the role. It was a perfect segway to the start of my nursing career. I landed the job after graduation and worked there until I passed the Nursing Council Licensure Exam (NCLEX), got my nursing license and secured a position at the local hospital—Halifax Medical Center. Indigo Manor is where I first witnessed transitional death. Meaning when terminal illness is determined, supportive care is provided-until death. A man was transitioning. Moving from the physical realm into a spiritual space that was defined by the religion he practiced-or didn't. I wondered where he was going or where his God told him he would. Hell or Heaven? Reincarnation? Would he come back as someone else? And if so, who from his formal physical life would he encounter, causing de ja vu?

I was in awe at the human body and how disease affected it. I had the same emotion about the end of life. The change in mentation, breathing, skin and the look of death. At the same time, I wondered if the person in transition felt any of the changes. Could they feel the loss of their physical being? Could they feel the labor of breathing as witnessed by those standing at their bedside? What did they see? Was it true that you see those who have passed before you, waiting for you in heaven? Could they hear their loved ones weeping in despair, wishing they could have one more day?

I was there when Babalu transitioned. Preceded by significant confusion, somnolence and then non-functional cardiac activity, Babalu took his last breath. He'd been sent to Jackson Memorial's emergency room by the nurses at the assisted living facility (ALF) he lived in. There was fear that he had a gastrointestinal bleed due to the blood thinners he was taking for a prior clot in his leg. The nurse alerted me of her suspicion and his whereabouts. I immediately called the ER to speak to Babalu's doctor. He confirmed the nurse's assessment and wanted to keep him for further monitoring, especially because he seemed to be confused-what we thought was due to the bleed and would resolve with treatment. That night, I went over to the hospital to visit with Babalu. I wanted to make sure he was properly taken care of. Being a healthcare provider, I'm aware of how the busi-ness of healthcare interferes with its care.

By the time I reached, Bablu was still in the ER, on a stretcher in the hallway. I hated this practice as a new nurse and even more 25 years later. It violates so many human principles-decency, privacy and respectability. Babalu seemed ok, though. He was aware of where he was and why. He even mentioned that he was going to stop drinking-as the doctor had recommended. I was shocked. One, because Babalu was giving up something that was a significant part of his identity. It was the way he'd made his living. It was the way he showed hospitality. Whenever anyone visited him at home or at the tree he hung out under, in his latter days, he'd ask, You wanna drink?". Shit, he'd even ask your underaged child if they wanted a drink and would gladly provide one. When we were kids, he'd give us a sip of Ole Milwaukee. Saying, "it'll kill da worms". I didn't know we had worms. LOL!

I was also surprised because Babalu was listening. I'd never known him to. Outwardly. He'd always done exactly what he wanted. No matter the consequences.

As our conversation ended and I gathered my things to leave, he asked that I bring him a cup of coffee when I returned the next morning. He loved coffee. As I do now. I can drink it all day. I love its taste and I love that Babalu loved it.

I responded with, "ok, I will." and told him that I would see him in the morning. Little did I know, that would be the last time I'd see him as Babalu. Lucid. Comical. Real.

The next morning came and Babalu was gone. As I'd known him. As we knew him. He was confused and ill appearing. I walked into his room and noticed his upper body wedged between the siderails and the mattress of his bed. His lower was in a side position. I imagine he was trying to get out of bed. Babalu was an early riser. So, his brain was prompting him to do as he normally did. Get up. His medical condition and the security of the siderails precluded the movement his brain was leading him to. I got closer and noticed him pulling at the air. As if he were grasping something. But there wasn't anything to grab. I called his name, and he didn't recognize me. I showed him the coffee he'd requested the night before. But nothing. He didn't reach for it. He just continued to grab for whatever he saw; the thing that was invisible to me. Several hours later, Babalu was transferred to the ICU. Septic. Unresponsive. Dying. The nurses and doctors worked on his physical to prevent transition into the spirit. They pressed on his chest. Gave him medicine. Shocked him. His physical never responded. I could see the team's efforts in the background as his doctor stood in my foreground. First, looking. Then asking, "Do you want us to continue?" I shifted my vision to him and them, pressing on his frail chest and forcing air into his lungs, manually. The monitor that displayed his vital signs that told me Babalu was no longer with me. He was gone, permanently. I then turned back to her, and said, "no".

Mourning, I stood over Babalu's lifeless body and wondered. What were his last lucid thoughts? Did he have any regrets? Did he want to tell me something but didn't have the energy to mouth the words? Was he in pain? Could he see our mother or his beloved brother, Bradley? Were they giving him the "ok" to leave? Or did he hear the music he created and loved in his head, while his brain gave his lungs their last cycles of ventilation? Was he singing "Bahamas Gone Independent" to himself, creating the joy so many experienced when he sang it aloud. I wondered.

I still do.

I passed the NCLEX.

As anticipated, I secured a job at Halifax Medical Center. The hospital was (and still is) in the heart of Daytona Beach, just off the speedway I'd travelled through 4 years prior. I was assigned to "10-East", Halifax's only non-ICU telemetry unit at the time. Telemetry is a mode of non-invasive cardiac monitoring that allows upfront visualization of the heart's electrical activity. The monitors display electrical conduction through a cadence of waves that peak and depress during the heart's cycles of contraction and relaxation. The heart rate, which is also displayed, tells how fast the heart goes through these cycles. In college I enjoyed learning the cardiovascular system the most. Comprised of blood vessels, electricity and muscle, each part is integral in its health and ensuring the health of all other organs. It feeds everything, including itself. Interesting how its physiology compares to its psychology. Without its primary connection, all we do, as humans, is meaningless. Some say, "the heart wants what the heart wants". I say, "the heart needs what the heart needs".

My shift was from 0700-1530 and I was making $13.01/hr. Nowadays, the only nurses working such short shifts are non-bedside nurses. Meaning the nurses aren't involved in direct patient care. They focus more on the quality or quantity of it-care management, utilization management, quality and risk management, clinical documentation improvement and nursing leadership. Also, the current average salary for entry-level nurses is \$23.69/hr. Damn. The entry-level salary still hasn't doubled. **It's only been 23 years** (input sarcasm)!

I'm amazed at how I survived on that low of a salary. My guess is that the general cost of living was more than affordable in Daytona Beach. But still. Since then, I've managed to do well for myself. I've soared through the profession, becoming an advanced practice nurse and now serving as a nurse leader. My salary has more than quadrupled and I'm in a career space I never could have imagined two decades ago.

Man, 10-East was something else. The unit was housed by patients suffering from acute cardiac problems and medical-surgical problems that could have a cardiac impact. 10-East is where my love of the cardiovascular system was confirmed. I carried out my first "code blue", burned my first patient by not diluting intravenous potassium, got cursed out by the attending cardiologist for not doing so, learned to read telemetry strips and met a lifetime friend-Dee.

Like me, Dee was a Capricorn. She was jovial, witty and would cuss you out as quickly as your eyes blinked. But would also give you her last dime-literally and figuratively. At the time we met, she was a (CNA) and had one son. He was about 5 or 6 at the time. When I saw her with her son, I knew why she worked so hard. To provide for him. I can see him now walking on the unit and breaking off running at the site of her. And then Dee would go to her locker to fetch a hairbrush. While stooping to his level, she'd hold his bottom jaw with one hand and brush his hair with the other. All while lovingly fussing and instructing him to be on his best behavior at the birthday party he was about to attend. And he, smiling through the entire encounter, nods and responds, "Ok Mommy."

Dee passed from metastatic, triple-negative breast cancer. I remember us talking early in her diagnosis. She was set on fighting the beast we all fear. Dee wanted continued life to finish her nurse practitioner degree, see her youngest son graduate from high school and help raise her grandchildren. At the time of her passing, her nurse practitioner degree was the only thing left undone. Life is so fucked up at times.

I love you Dee. Always!!

10-East is also where I started to see how my character would challenge me for years to come.

My nurse manager was Cookie Moore. Ms. Moore is what she demanded to be called. She stood about 5'1" and had relaxed hair that obviously sat in sponge rollers the night before. Her curls were unbothered. Her face was bare, except for a perfectly fitted pair of squared, silver glasses. She wore a traditional nursing uniform. You know-a crisp white top, tucked into a crisp white skirt that fell well below her knees. You could hear her coming before you saw her by the sound of the tights that scrubbed together due to the habitus of her thighs. And you know her shoes were cocaine white. I could tell she routinely used Kiwi shoe polish to refurbish the color. There were hints of old shoe polish contrasted by the newest strokes she'd applied. Ms. Moore did not smile. And neither did I. I remember our first run-in. I was sitting in the nursing station, cross-checking physicians' orders. Back then, physicians would handwrite their orders on paper, and fold them in a triangle, alerting the nurse to the new orders. The nurse would then review the orders and initial them, attesting to the order review and completion. As I'm doing so, the phone rings. Ms. Moore was standing on the other side of the nursing station and directed me to answer the phone. I looked up at her to say" aren't you standing there?" and proceeded to check off my orders. She answered the phone, finished the call and then requested that I come to her office. "Here we go with this bullshit", I'm saying to myself.

She opened her door, sat behind her desk and I sat across from her. Ms. Moore had a quiet subtle voice, so you had to really pay attention when she spoke. She asked, "Why didn't you answer the phone?". I responded, "Because I was checking off my orders." She goes on, "But I asked you to answer it." And I go on, "And I was busy. Why couldn't you answer it? You were standing right there." I said this while looking at her, straight on, into her eyes. After I said what I said, I fell silent. She didn't continue our conversation. "You can go", she said. I got up, opened the door and asked, "You want it opened or closed?" "Closed, please.", Ms. Moore replied.

I went on about my workday and didn't think twice about what had just happened. I'm sure Ms. Moore immediately picked up the phone and called her closest co-worker-going on and on about my insubordination and what she likely considered insolence. Without knowing, I was creating a reputation for myself that would follow me through my time at Halifax and beyond.

I had a similar experience in college. I was sitting with my new friends in the lounge area of our dorm-telling and comparing stories of old. We were going on and on about where we were from, whose city or state was the best, and if someone was from the hood-what struggles we endured. And the more the stories flowed, the louder we got. Especially me. I, then, and now have an alto tone of voice. It's not like my friend Sandra's voice- soft and sweet. Almost baby-like. I would say mine is more like Angela Basset's voice-strong, with a hint of sweetness. Just a hint. And I had (still do) a boisterous laugh. So, you can imagine how my voice and laughs intensified as the conversations did. Conscious of how loud we were, I would subtly check in with our dorm manager to see how she was responding to our noise levels. I was sitting in the center of the room, with a straight-on view of her office, which is where she sat for the entirety of her shift. I would gauge her temperament by her facial expressions. She was a fair-skinned, middle-aged black woman with a natural frown. You know how the ends of some people's mouths hang downward? Well, that's how her mouth had settled. She always appeared upset, or non-approachable- as people so often call me. If at any point I saw wrinkles in her forehead or saw her head shake in disagreement, I'd have everyone lower their voice; showing that I was in tune with her and that I was being respectful.

Then I noticed her leaving her office and walking towards the group. As she approached, everyone silenced themselves. And as our mouths closed, our postures improved. I'm always in awe of how our brains interpret behaviors and the immediate physiologic responses that follow. You see this in the fight or flight response to trouble and in those who have experienced trauma. The minute those experiences present themselves, our hearts respond first-ensuring we have enough blood flow to protect ourselves in whooping a muthahfucka's ass or hauling ass. And in trauma the same.

She stood in the middle of the group, looked at me and said, "You're too loud." Now you know... I think you have an idea of my temperament by now. I immediately took offense to her addressing me and not the group. Especially when I was the one managing the group to avoid such an encounter. I asked, "Why are you singling me out, there are 6 other people here". She responds, "You're the loudest". Well, I'll be damned, I thought and spoke. And of course, she took offense. "What did you say?" "I mean, there are 6 people sitting here and you focusing on me. I don't understand", I responded. Meanwhile, the group is looking at me like, "Girl, shut the fuck up. You gon get us all in trouble." She asked us to leave the lounge and return to our rooms. We complied.

The next day, I was called to The Dean of Women's Office-Dean Sedona. Again, I had no idea of how the evening before would affect me, and neither did I think there would be any repercussions to my actions. I went to her office and checked in with the secretary, who escorted me to her formal office.

The Dean was sitting behind her big ass mahogany desk, with her big ass afro, dark lips and fingertip-like she either smoked weed or Benson and Hedges Menthol cigarettes all her life. "Dean, Ms. Nesbitt is here", said the secretary. She extended her hand toward the chair positioned in front of the Dean's desk, suggesting that I have a seat and exited the office. I sit, the Dean clasps her hands and does not crack a smile. She got straight to the point. "What happened between you and Ms. Calor last evening?" I respond, "huh". "What happened between you and Ms. Calor last night?" I say, "nothin". "Well, something must have happened, because she called me very upset, saying how disrespectful you were." I sit back in my chair, cross my arms and shake my head in disbelief. "This woman went crying to the Dean when she was the one that was dead ass wrong", I thought.

Dean Sedona went on to tell me how disrespectful I was and that my attitude would not be tolerated. I had nothing to say. Ms. Calor had obviously only conveyed part of our conversation and failed to fully disclose the circumstances of the evening. And it was also clear to me that Dean Sedona believed everything she said. Then she said something that made my heart drop. "For the remaining semester, you will live in Joyner Hall." "Huh", I replied. "Yes, your dorm assignment will be changed. You will need to move, imme-diately." I was devastated. This wasn't like being grounded by your parents. Her decision was a jail sentence. She was taking me away from my friends and the comfort of my home. And the dorm I was re-assigned to, Joyner Hall, was a dump. It looked old, smelled old and the bathrooms were shared with everyone that lived on the floor. Like the ones you've either used (For those that have spent some time-no judgment here) or seen in jails. Stalls. Ass and Titties out. No shower curtains. Just air and stank coochies. And to top it off, the girls of Joyner Hall clearly skipped "Hygiene and Clean Up After Your Damn Self" 101. The toilets were filled with shit and piss and the shower stalls were left with remnants of their monthlies! I was distraught. I knew all of this before moving cause I visited a friend or two that lived in Joyner Hall. And after every visit, I thanked Jesus that I didn't have live under such conditions.

I moved.

I can't tell you who my roommate was or what room I was assigned to. I aint even wanna know while I was living there. I do remember being on the first floor, though. And my bed was the one closest to the entry door.

I was despondent. This was the first time I thought, "You should have kept your damn mouth shut!" I was striken with regret. I would not accept the re-assignment in permanence. The only thing I would accept were two release dates-mine and Mary J.'s "My Life". It was the one thing that got me through the punishment. If you're familiar with the album, you know Mary was going through a hard time in her life. Her struggle with substance and her relationship with Mr. "Oooh-Yeah", got her thinking about Her Life. She sang through hurt and the last places she felt it. "In the background of Roy Ayers' "Everybody Loves the Sunshine", you can hear Mary's alto voice in the foreground-

"If you look at my life, you'll see what I see. Lah-dah-dah-dah. "If you look at my life, you'll see what I see. Lah-dah-dah-dah. "If you look at my life, you'll see what I see. Lah-dah-dah-dah. Life can be only what you make it. When you're feeling down, you should never fake it. Say what's on your mind and you and you'll find in time that all the negative energy, it will all cease."

The "key" to the song was my life being what I made it. I'd always lived this way, but never "actually" thought about it. Although I was punished, unfairly, I had to make the best of the situation and move on. "Mind over matter". Dean Sedona could put me in a cage but couldn't cage my mind. And Mary's My Life Album was the "best" of that point in my life. I eventually completed my sentence and was released home to LLC. (I wrote that like I sat in TGK for a year!!)

Given my response to Ms. Moore and Calor, one could easily say that I didn't respect authority. That I was unmanageable. I respected and respect authority. But I, too, had been authority. And still am. So, following instructions of an "actual" authoritative figure was a complicated ask for me. And still is. I say this in hindsight, of course. I didn't think I required managing. I'd been the top manager-of my siblings, our house and my life. So, what could anyone tell me? I'd become a super adult and I saw my superiors as peers. Now, please don't misunderstand me. I was fearful of police and going to jail. And I was afraid of my dad-at a point. But the "powers" would always be thrown at me countering their decisions when I sensed they were being unreasonable or unfair. This happened with Babalu, causing him to put me out the house and tell me that I'd be worse off when I left his safe keeping than I was under it. And the same with most of my romantic relationships. Men assume power-culturally, in their minds, family and relationships. Some take on that assumption with pride and manage it well. While others abuse it. It becomes their ego. And so happened, these are the men I had major romances with. This is the man I married.

CHAPTER 9

THE TRANSITION

I'm writing this book more than 4 decades after my initial life insults. And for the last 3 decades, those insults have showed up in my life in ways I didn't realize until now. Rather, they've caused me to show up "Hurt".

I was "laid off" my job.

A year prior, my ex-husband and I moved to Ft. Worth, Texas (from Houston) for the job. And exactly a year later, it was eliminated. The week of my layoff, I noticed that I was being excluded from meetings where my input as the meeting's subject business owner was integral. I could feel it. My peers were responding to me differently. They were quiet. Almost sullen. The final straw broke when I attended a meeting, that again, I wasn't invited to. Immediately after, I received a call from my boss telling me not to attend any meetings unless I was instructed. I was paralyzed in thought. I didn't understand. "Why is this happening", I thought. "And when did leaders start uninviting leaders to meetings?" I'd never experienced anything like this. Mind you, I'd just buried my brother a month prior and had broken my arm a month prior to that. I was on the verge of a nervous breakdown. "How much can a bitch take", I thought. I immediately contacted Darlene. She was one of my directors and I admired a great deal. We'd grown close professionally and personally. I texted her, "How about this muthahfuckah called to tell me not to go to the clinical meeting?" She responds, "Who?" I respond, "Moriah." She responds, "Unbelievable."

Needing to act quickly, I stopped texting Darlene and emailed my administrative assistant, Frenchy, asking her to come to my office. Hearing the urgency in my message, she got there in lightning speed. My door was cracked, so she peeked her head in to see if it was ok to enter. I was so upset, I couldn't speak. As soon as she came in, Frenchy could see the expression on my face. I was drunk in sorrow. "What's wrong", Frenchy asked, in the sweetest voice. She always spoke this way. Anytime you saw Frenchy, she offered the most genuine smile. You couldn't help but smile back. She made you feel happy just because she was happy.

"I think they're trying to get rid of me. I've been excluded from meetings; they've invited Darlene and Celeste to the division meeting and to the upcoming retreat. They are preparing to let me go." Frenchy responds, "I knew there was something up. I noticed the last-minute invitations. And the HR Director cancelled your meeting late last night." That's all I needed to hear. Frenchy confirmed my fears. I was being fired. But I didn't understand. Although I'd only been with the company a short time, I'd done an excellent job. The department was thriving. It was better organized, and I'd come up with improvement strategies my predecessors hadn't. Also, team rapport had improved, and I'd saved millions of dollars in revenue within months. And to add, my performance was evaluated as "proficient". I had no documented performance improvement plan. So, why were they treating me this way?

I told Frenchy to gather my immediate belongings and bag them so that I could put them in my car, first thing, the next morning. Then I grabbed my bag and keys and went home. I called my husband, Otunde, on the way. As I dialed his number, I asked myself, "Bitch, why are you calling him? You know he will not empathize and probably feels the same way the muthahfuckahs at the job feel."

By now, my ex-husband was explicit in how he saw and experienced me. To him, I was-emotionally immature, a narcissist, righteous, a hypocrite and manly. I'd gained these descriptors through the many arguments we had over our three-year relationship. The most hurtful was "manly". He'd say, "You want to be the man of this relationship." That statement struck a nerve at the bottom of my soul. If you can imagine souls having nerves, that's how deep, "you wanna be the man", went for me. Back then, I couldn't fully articulate why I felt the way I did. I know it hurt, partly, because it showed how much I was misunderstood. Like Ms. Calor, Dean Sedona and many others, Otunde interpreted the certainties and convictions I held about myself as insubordination. He, nor they, considered the "why" of me. But Otunde was supposed to. I was his wife. He felt like he understood and would often say, "believe me, I understand you." How could he, though? He almost never asked questions about my parents, my upbringing, or my childhood. He never asked my opinion or for insight. He only injected his every chance he got and would get frustrated if I thought differently. Outside of me being a nurse, he couldn't articulate what I did for a living. He never asked. And when I asked about him not asking, he would always respond, "I don't need to ask questions to know you. I'll learn as I go." He'd also say, "If you want me to know something, you'll tell me." His approach did not impart interest. It only reminded me of how I was treated as a child. Invisibly.

Maybe Otunde did understand me. Maybe he knew where I was last hurt. At times I feel like he used the parts of my life that crushed me most as leverage to make me feel and believe that I'd never be whole. And if I wasn't, I wouldn't go anywhere because no one would want me. Or I'd feel like he was the best I could do, keeping me stuck in a relationship with him. He never minded throwing the lowest of insults. And then act as if he never mumbled a harmful word. I'd always ask, "If I'm this, then why are you with me?" "Why would you want to be with a narcissist or a hypocrite?" He'd respond, "Because I love you." That never registered with me. Or maybe it did. I was damn shole conditioned to being abused by my protectors. People that made, birthed and harmed me at the same time. Maybe I felt right at home with Otunde. Maybe I felt like I did when I was home with Babalu.

I should have asked myself, "Why do you stay?" My answer now, "because I didn't know I was stuck."

I called. And I was right. After listening to my frustrated voice, his only offering was that I "play the game". Not "I'm sorry babe." Not, "I can't believe them muthahuckas let you go." But "you gotta play the game."

The next day I arrived at work early enough to gather the items Frenchy had packed. I immediately took them to my car. I didn't want HR packing my personal belongings. You know- the bills that I paid during work downtime and the checks that I E-deposited. I also had a few travel coffee containers and a waist trainer that I'd worn several months prior. It was so uncomfortable that I took the bitch off and sat it at the bottom of my desk drawer. I'm sure Frenchy got a good chuckle when she discovered it.

Once I returned to the office, I quickly gathered my team. I wanted to let them know what was about to happen. I had to tell the story from my perspective. I had to tell the truth. Otherwise, the explanation of my exit is left to the C-Suite. They are notorious for letting you go and then sending a bullshit ass email afterwards, citing your egress being due to new opportunities. Or they'd just say, "effectively immediately", your ass ain't there no more, which usually happens when you've cussed someone out (likely long overdue and well deserved), or when you are a cultural misfit. Otherwise, you're celebrated with an hour of tributes from fellow co-workers, followed by cake and chicken wings in the common office meeting area. And if you were part of the elite, you get a night out that included food and drinks at a nearby restaurant.

Mid-day, I was invited to my boss' office. Upon arrival, she was sitting behind her desk (sound familiar?) and accompanied by an unidentified woman with a bob. I'd been here before, so I knew what was up. My boss started talking and I checked out. I interrupted her mid-sentence, telling her she didn't need to go through the formalities, cause I knew what I was there for. So, she could cut the shit. She stopped talking and left the office. Then the lady with the bob took her seat. She started to blabber about my role being eliminated, me having 30 days to find another job within the company and that the meeting was my formal notice. "Eliminated, 30 days, notice?!", I thought. Why would a role so integral to the company be eliminat-ed? And why were they giving me 30 days to find a job at the same company, especially when they know damn well I wouldn't "fit" in any other role. And if I had 30 days to find a job, why did I have to leave immediately? And why did the lady with the bob need my badge? And why did I couldn't I go back to my office to retrieve my belongings? Why?

I was their cultural mis-fit. They didn't like my character, and elim-inating my role was an underhanded, passive-aggressive way to fire me without doing so. This was also their way of avoiding litigation. My role elimination was a way to communicate their disdain for my lack of "collaboration" and for being "unapproachable." All labels they'd given me because I didn't assimilate to corporate culture. Be-cause I made my own decisions-when theirs was unreasonable and unfair. Because they didn't know that my parents made me a super adult, decades prior. Which meant that I saw them as my peers, not my authority. They did the same thing that Ms. Moore did when she quietly whispered to her peers at Halifax-defaming my professional character. And Ms. Calor and Dean Sedona, when they sentenced me to Joyner Hall. And my husband. When he labelled me as hypocriti-cal, too driven and narcissistic. And when he broke my arm.

Losing my job saddened me. While I did not drop a tear in front of my team or those who let me go, I cried a river at home. I was inconsolable. I felt broken. Worthless-like a penny with a hole in it. My career was the one thing I felt successful at. It was the result of the things I was acknowledged for as a child-responsibility and edu-cation. It was my "one true thing". Imagine the confusion of being praised for something for one part of your life and then discarded for the same. Ms. Moore, my ex-husband, Dean Sedona and Ms. Cal-or didn't consider the traits driving my success in education and ca-reer to be the same for all things in life. There was no switch. No, be one way over here and then change it over there. Some men expect this degree of metamorphosis from black women. We, women, have evolved out of the traditional roles our mothers and grandmothers once filled, into roles historically filled by men. We were once sole domesticators-cooking cleaning, carrying and caring for our babies.

And now, we hire cooks, cleaners and someone to carry and care for our babies. Men's roles have remained static. And I believe they look for women's roles to do the same, despite obvious progression. The desire doesn't come from malice (for the most part), but from who men are and have allowed to be naturally-leaders, protectors and providers. They're also used to the balance women bring with our softer, nurturing tendencies. Unfortunately, our now dynamic roles preclude these inclinations and move us more towards what's expected of a man. As a result, men feel useless, and emasculated.

I'm sure this is what Otunde felt and experienced with me, causing him to make comments about my "manliness". And the same for the other authoritative figures I've had untoward experiences with. Even if they were women. Traditionally, authority equals man. And protest is not allowed. Especially from a woman. When this happens, the woman is put in what's supposed to be her place through punishment, labeling and micro-aggressions. But for women like me, methods used to put me in my place are met with defense. I, then, become even more manly.

This was not the first time I was fired. It was the 4th time. Two were outright and the others were covert. My first termination was from a job in Atlanta. I was practicing as a Nurse Practitioner in a city just north of what's "properly" considered Atlanta. Nurse Practitioners are clinical nurses trained to practice nursing at an advanced level. A great deal of the training mimics medical doctors' training-diagnosis and treatment of medical illnesses as well as medication prescription. Some even carry out minor surgical procedures.

I had come upon my clinic rotation, which required me to work in the office. I was responsible for new patients and follow-up visits. So, if your primary care physician thought it was necessary for you to see a cardiologist, there was a good chance you'd be seen by me. And if you were established with one of the practice physicians, there was an even greater chance that you'd end up in one of my visit slots.

New patient visits were carried out more carefully than established visits. The provider would have to understand the patient's entire health history, including family history, medications, social habits, allergies and procedures. Then, consider the reason for the referral, how the prior medical history contributes, finalize a diagnosis and come up with a treatment plan. This could take up to an hour, or more, depending on the complexity of the patient. What was even more time-intensive was reconciling a new patient's medications. Many would come with grocery bags of medications that were pre-scribed over time. Either by their primary care physician, other con-sulting physicians or hospital physicians. Several medications were duplicative. The patient didn't know because one medicine would be provided in the brand name and the other in the generic name.

One day, in the clinic, my slots seemed to be filled with all new patients. And as the day went on, more were added. Knowing what it took to complete a comprehensive visit, there was no way to keep up with the demand. So, I called the receptionist and asked that she stop adding patients to my schedule. I explained that my slots were filled with new patients, and I didn't have time to take on any more. She seemingly obliged. About an hour later, I got a call from the same receptionist. "Hey Charkes, Mona would like to see you in her office." Mona was the office manager. "Oh Lord", I thought. "Here we go with this bullshit, again." As I sauntered to her office, I ask myself, "Girl, why are you always being called to the principal's of-fice"? Then I say to myself, "The hell if I know." I felt like the lit-tle girl reporting to Mr. Mingo's office in elementary school to get paddled for excessive talking. Yes, that was a thing. And I have no complaints about it.

I get to Mona's, sit and wait for her to speak. She politely asked me why I asked the receptionist to stop adding patients to my schedule. I told her that I was overwhelmed with new patients and wouldn't be able to see any more beyond what was scheduled. Her response was, "You can't do that." "You can't stop patients from being added to your schedule." My thoughts, "Well I obviously can, 'cause I did." As Mona continued to present my wrongdoings, Mr. Carey walked in and sat next to me. He was the CEO of the company. Mr. Carey stood average in height, had a thick head of dirty blonde hair, that was thickest at his forehead and signed his name with a green pen.

I remember asking him why he preferred green ink. His response, "because it doesn't photocopy." At that point, I should have known he couldn't be trusted. With his right leg crossed over the left, and his hands clasped at the top of his right knee, he looked my way and asked what happened during my night shift rotation at the hospital. I asked him to clarify because there were several occurrences during those three nights. Somebody called because they ran out of Lopressor, two people had chest pain, and another forgot to take Coumadin for 5 days. So, he needed to be a little more specific. He explained that a partnering surgeon sent a patient over to the emergency room due to an abnormal EKG and I refused to admit the patient. Immediately, I remembered the patient and recalled what happened. I told him that the patient recently had surgery and that I did not feel comfortable admitting but would consult due to the abnormal EKG. Admitting the patient would make me solely responsible for all that was the matter with him. And because I was not his surgeon or a part of his surgical team, I wasn't willing to take on such responsibility. I could comfortably assist with any cardiovascular issue causing the abnormal EKG. Mr. Carey listened intently, making sure to have eye contact as I spoke. And I made sure I did the same, wanting to ensure he could trust what I was saying. Mr. Carey looked confused about my explanation. His forehead wrinkled like I said something wrong. He went on to tell me that he'd recently started a partnership with that surgeon, and I'd jeopardized that relationship by not admitting the patient. I then realized the wrinkles in his forehead didn't represent confusion, they were his response to my disobedience… insubordination. This conversation was familiar to me. I'd been here before. Several times. Charkes, again, was challenging authority. But the difference here was that I had the slightest of clues about the agreement he spoke of. Not that having this information would have changed my decision. But I would have known what I was up against in doing so. After a brief pause, I asked Mr. Carey if I could ask him a question. He responded, "Sure". I glanced over at the degree on the wall in front of me and noticed it was his; awarded for studies in business administration from Kennestone State University. We were sitting in his office, not Mona's. I asked him what his degree was in. He responded, "Business". I say, "ok and mine is in medicine." So, if you don't mind, let me manage medicine and you manage business. My naivety didn't allow me to understand that he was managing a business. The business of healthcare. I saw them as exclusives, and he saw them as one and the same. I was terminated the next day.

One would say I should have just taken responsibility for the patient and kept my mouth shut. Play "The Game". Back then, I didn't know what The Game was and am still confused about it more than a decade later. Part of what I understand about The Game is that a great deal of success is determined by likeability. People must like you to be comfortable with you. If not, the probability of discard and ostracism is high. People like what is similar. What is familiar. Looking the same racially, behaving the same culturally, and earning the same financially makes one indistinguishable. This makes people feel safe. And safety makes all of us comfortable, including me. But I also had no issue being different. My temperament and approach to life caused me to lean more towards differentiality. So being different was comfortable to me.

Likeability also has to do with not reminding people of their insecurities. Not being sure of yourself because the person you're relating to is unsure. Not dressing attractively because the person on the other side doesn't have the taste in style to. Not boasting about your relationship because the other person's relationship failed. Not being knowledgeable because the other person is ill informed. Don't misunderstand my position. This has nothing to do with the "seemingly" secure person. Most times. But when one is reminded of how they are less than, or their perception of themselves in that way, crushing ensues. This is why it's key to take time to understand people and yourself. Doing so allows considerable interactions. You become aware of how you show up and how you'll be perceived and received by the other party. The goal is to leave people better than you found them, and the same for you. I didn't learn this until late in life. Actually, a couple of years ago. My ex- husband's physical response to me made me realize the dissonance in who I was and who he perceived me to be.

The Game is also taught at an early age. I believe those who are best at it grew up or spent time in certain environments, allowing acceptance of the mindset and culture with ease. For example, if you grew up in a home where one or both parents worked corporate jobs, you were given a head start in corporate culture. You've overheard the conversations, seen the dress style, felt the posture and grew to understand the ladder and how to navigate it. I only knew education, work ethic and integrity to be the driving forces in success. Nobody told me about the other stuff. As time went on, in my career and personal life, I learned what I didn't know. The Game. I learned that I didn't fit the bill through, "You're unapproachable." "You're not collaborative." "You're a know-it-all." "You're defensive." "You're intimidating". Corporate culture is extremely sensitive to those that don't fit. And when you don't, the labels start flying. Or as they call it now, "micro-aggression". I've experienced the same in my romantic relationships, which is comparable because men are typically seen as the powerful ones in corporate and American culture. With Otunde, if I stood too tall, he'd name call so that I would sit down. If I thought too much, he'd argue with me, so that I wouldn't think at all (for myself). If I dreamed too big, he'd tell me that I was delusional. And If I felt too much, he'd say I was emotionally immature.

With my career and marriage on the brink, it was time for me to transition.

CHAPTER 10:

STRONG

Growing up in Liberty City, Florida, in the 80s and 90s was no easy feat. If you're not familiar with the area, check the archives of "The First 48". I'm positive the city was featured a dozen times or more. "The City" as natives refer to it, was comprised of lower-class neighborhoods where residents lived to check, no check, or survived on low-income housing and food stamps. The communities were overwhelmed with prostitution, alcoholism, and drug addiction. Well, at least that's what my siblings and I experienced. I'm sure you've heard these details from tons of people you know, or maybe you lived in one of these hellholes yourself. And if so, you know that only the strong survive and survival doesn't always mean that you come out shiny on the other end.

The City and my parents made my formative years tough. My mother and father gave life to 9 children, but never married. Most of their children were a year apart, except for my brother Keo and I; we are 10 months apart. I was born in January, and he was born in November of the same year. Oh, and Duke was born 2 years after us. I guess our mom needed a break. Yolanda Yvette Buford was her name. My siblings and I called her "Ya-Yow". It was our version of "Yo-Yo", which is what she was called by her family. Ya-Yow only had a high school education. And while I don't know the details of her early life, the choices she made reflected that of a woman in search of herself-through acceptance and love of a man. I identify with this because this is me. I have related to my mother in more ways than I care to admit. Her desire for and response to my father was intense. So intense, it caused her to neglect herself and her children. I've been there and done the same. Neglected myself and Adrian for a relationship that ended up neglecting, and then discarding, both he and I. You've been reading about my experiences with men. One after the other, making the same bad decisions, for the same reasons-acceptance and love. And when I don't get either, I'm hurt. And then stuck where I was last hurt, but in a different situation.

I imagine my mom and dad having a whirlwind love affair. Like the ones I've had. He was a handsome, charismatic, foreign musician who migrated to the United States and settled in Miami. I heard that they met at his nightclub, where my mom would hang out from time to time. I don't know the true story of their meeting, and then, union. So, I must settle for what I've made up in my mind knowing them both. I imagine him being extremely attracted to her. She was about 5'11, with light skin and an unforgettable smile. Seriously, it was big, wide and beautiful. Breathtaking. Her buoyant energy, full lips and beautiful teeth added to the sexiness of her body. She had legs and hips for days and curves that women pay good money for now. This depiction is extremely different when compared to her last living years. There's a picture of my mom sitting in a wheelchair, in multiple layers of clothes. Her skin was impregnated with Kaposi's Sarcoma. Her top two front teeth were missing, permanently damaging the smile she was known for. Her curves withered to mush. Her energy was reserved for recuperation from dialysis sessions and moving from bed to chair due to advanced heart failure. She was dying of AIDS.

My first and most clear memories of my parents are filled with sex, fights, and sadness. She was always running behind him, begging him to see her, even with babies in tow. One inside and the other on her hip. And he was always beating her because she interfered with the life he'd set for himself. One where his band, nightclub and women were priority; not her, the hurt she came with or the 9 children she would bare. As time went on, my mother's mind grew tired. Their relationship was toxic, and childbearing wreaked havoc on her body. She stopped caring. Her deep desire for him caused her to neglect herself and us, forcing child protective services to step in. We became foster kids and were nearly adopted before we went back to our parents. When I noticed my mom again, she was withdrawn and depressed. She barely spoke, except for when she was talking to herself. We could no longer depend on her to protect us physically because she wasn't safe mentally. She was eventually deemed unfit and was sent away. I, then, had to fill her vacancy. I was in primary school, not even reaching puberty yet.

I share the details of my formative years in my first book, *"1177: Undaunted"*. This work was a means of cleansing and a way to help others see their lives and potential through me. I claimed that the book lent to the understanding of life not having to be the sum of your worst circumstances. But I sit here, 7 years later, wondering if that is true. I wonder if my life is reflective of something other than the trauma I'd endured as a child. I wonder if I am the storm of my mother and father's personalities, decisions and lingering insecurities. These thoughts beg themselves in every aspect of my life. As a mother, a sister, a leader and an ex-wife. The life they forced me into has infiltrated my being for the past 26 years, causing both success and stagnation. Causing me to be strong while weak. Causing me to be stuck where I was last hurt.

The word "strong" has many definitions. According to Webster, strong can mean the power to move heavy weights or perform other physically demanding tasks. It also means possessing skills and qualities that create a likelihood of success, or powerfully affecting the mind senses or emotions. There are a few others. I've used the last two definitions to explain how "strong" has showed up in my life and why. My earliest memories have resurfaced, and the connected those experiences with who I am now, in a cause-and-effect manner. These memories have showed how hurt I was when I moved. I was moving while stagnant. I was strong while weak.

The way my parents went about their lives did not create safe spaces for any of us. There were no healthy standards for love or esteem; and the blueprints they created almost guaranteed failure. While my father had been married twice before meeting my mother, he never married her. He always had a side piece driving my mother's depression into full speed. Although he wasn't to blame, totally, for her psychological friability; his behavior watered it. He was never home, and she made it a point to be wherever he was to "piss on his leg"-thwarting off any potential lovers. They carried on this way, all while having children. Nine of them. As time passed, our minds were being conditioned to dysfunction as the norm. We were born and bred in trauma, lovelessness, and sorrow, and would not see the full manifestations of these circumstances until decades later.

One of my first memories of my mother was her leaving me home alone. I've told this story numerous times and written it at least three. I had to be about 5 or 6 years old. We were living in an upper-level apartment. I know this to be true because I also remember a time when I got stuck in between the apartment's elevator door.

While sitting on the living room floor, I could hear her in the bathroom getting ready while singing along with one of her favorites, Stephanie Mills. She appeared from the bathroom and disappeared at the same time. She walked past me, right out the front door. I'm sure she was going to my dad's nightclub to sit at the bar and start her "pissing" session. I cried like the baby I was, wondering why she would leave me alone. Grant it, there could have been someone babysitting. But I don't remember anyone else but her. Walking out, she didn't pick me up to say, "I'll be right back". She didn't ask me if I wanted to go with her. And neither did she kiss me before she left. This behavior continued for years, even while birthing more children. The only difference was that I was left behind attending to my siblings.

As a child, I cooked, laundered clothes, combed hair, granted permission to play outside and beckoned them in when playtime was over. I made sure they got up in time for school and walked alongside them as we all went to school. I protected them the best I could. These experiences made me responsible, nurturing, caring, understanding and mature-even before I knew what all of that meant. As a child, I'd possessed all the characteristics needed to be a mother to my own son, a mentor to those who would suffer from the same travesties I suffered and the independence and boldness I needed as a professional. These experiences made me STRONG.

Three decades later, I am the mother of a 23-year-old man, hold undergraduate and graduate degrees in Nursing, and for the last 10 years, have served as a senior leader in Hospital Clinical Resource Management. A field I didn't even know existed during my undergraduate studies. I am a personal and professional mentor. I've authored and published two books. This is my third. And on the verge of launching a life coaching business. My former years have folded into my now years making me STRONGER!

But what's on the other side of the experiences that made me strong? Aside from the successes, what else did they produce? What have they caused? Yes, the earliest years of my life cultivated know-how, fearlessness, and resilience. Strength. But at the same time, it created fear, self-doubt, pain and trauma. Fear of rejection-because I was rejected by my parents. They didn't make sure I was taken care of but surely made sure I took care of their responsibilities. Self-doubt because I was never affirmed. No conversations telling me, "I'm kind, I'm pretty or enough", just pain from physical and emotional abuse and neglect. My mother would beat the shit out because she was angry with herself, her mother and all the men that let her down, including my father.

Parents are responsible for their children's well-being, sense of self-worth, and acceptance, at least in the formative years. They help build character. But when you struggle, as an adult parent, with well-being, self-worth, and acceptance, the space from which you lend to your child's character is underdeveloped, and even absent, in some instances. The space is cloudy, ashen, and torn in little pieces. So how on earth are you to example any resemblance of health to your offspring? One's reproductive ability is not precluded by their innermost malignant states. What ends up happening is that your children become products of your deepest environments and the worst parts of you. And then you send them off into the world to perform your scripts of maladjustment.

CHAPTER 11:

FAMILIARITY

I met him 4 years ago. We got married a year ago and divorced exactly a week prior to typing these words. He was dark, bearded and handsome. He was foreign. He was charismatic. His name. His heritage. His way. Foreign. Yet so familiar. I liken what my eyes saw, in him, to that of the man I'd looked upon for most of my life. My father.

He, too, was dark-skinned, handsome, charismatic and a foreigner. An immigrant from the Bahamas, Edison Nesbitt, Sr. (Babalu) was everything a woman wanted outwardly. He was "The People's Person". He was an entrepreneur. A musician. Songwriter. Percussionist. A Singer. You can find two of his records, "Calypso Funk" and "Bahamas Gone Independent" on YouTube. Though recorded long before I was born, Babalu would perform these songs on his very own stage, at his night club, "The Banana Boat." And if your parents traversed Miami's party scene during the late 70s and early 80's, they may have heard about my dad or had a night out, featuring Babalu.

I remember the first time I saw him perform. I've told this story in my first book. And I'll tell it here. I heard him before I could see him. And when I saw him, I could feel his love for music, entertainment, and people. I couldn't...they couldn't...help but love Babalu. He's been gone for almost 7 years now. But whenever his friends speak of him, they do with respect, joy and laughter. They recall stories that illuminate his way, his character, and his thoughts. They remember the way they danced to the sound of his voice and the thumping cadence of his drums. They remember his friendship. They loved him for the same reasons I did. For him.

I also remember Babalu's eyes. I remember them when he was in a good mood. When he was joking or pranking. I remember them when he would play "Catch the Dollar" with us. We would have to position our hands with our thumb and index finger ready to catch the dollar bill he would let fall, unexpectedly, from his hands. You could keep all the dollars you caught. I remember his eyes when commenting about the way someone looked, a person's response to situations or even farting. Babalu's farts were always silent, but deadly, which he found amusing. His farts smelled like someone had literally crawled up his ass and died. They were obnoxious. Putrid. Decades ago, Babalu had undergone a gastrointestinal procedure, resulting in the need for an ostomy. Knowing what I know now, most of his large intestine was removed, leaving his small intestine to fend for itself in absorption and elimination.

Babalu's eyes, when he was not on stage, in a crowd or amongst friends, were different. They were stern, inflexible and mean. I remember them because I saw them the most. He used them when dictating responsibilities for children that weren't my own. He used them when barking orders about cleaning, and cooking. He used them when waking me up in the wee hours of the morning, before school, to wash clothes. For him, this was the most sensible time to do laundry, as he'd been at The Banana Boat hours prior. He used these eyes when giving my brother Keo and I instructions on how to sweep and mop spillings of Guinness, Old Milwaukee, and Michelob from The Banana Boat's floors. And, when wiping Benson and Hedges ashes from the square tables and plastic ashtrays. I remember those eyes, and unbeknownst to me, I would see them again. In someone else. My ex-husband.

After 8 months of a long-distance romance, I moved. I resigned from the job I long for now, deserted my child and left my family and friends behind. All for him. For the long-awaited relationship. The relationship, I thought would finally fill me up, making me whole.

The relationship we girls are taught to dream of as our lives. The relationship Steveland Morris sings about in "Overjoyed".

> *"Over time, I've been building my castle of love. Just for two. Though you never knew you were my reason. I've gone much too far, for you now to say, that I've got to throw my castle away." ..." And though you don't believe that they do, they do come true, for did my dreams come true when I looked at you. And maybe too if you would believe, you too might be overjoyed, and over-loved over me."*

I remember my bosses questioning my decision. One asked, "Is he worth all of this"? And the other asked, "What is so great about him that you would change your life around in such a way?" My response was, "Yes, he is." And "He takes care of me." "He makes sure I'm ok." They both shook their heads in disbelief. He was the one. And then he wasn't.

Weeks after moving to Texas, we ventured to Dubai together. We'd decided on the trip months prior, when I was still living in Florida. Excitedly, I contacted my travel agent, and she made it happen. I'd chosen from the list of recommended hotels and "things to do". He never seemed difficult while planning. He pretty much went along with whatever I was good with. "Wow", I thought. And he paid his half...I was amazed. I know what you're thinking, "You excited about a negro paying his half of a trip he's going on." Yep. You're right. Those were my standards, though. Anyone doing what was expected superseded what I was used to.

Life was perfect. We traveled without incident. We slept, cuddling the best way we could, given our coach seating. And after the 13-hour Emirates flight, we finally arrived. Then, he wanted to walk to the liquor store. My immediate thoughts, "We are in a foreign country, with funky Google Maps directions, and it's dark outside." "And sidewalks are scarce." "Why is he so pressed to find a liquor store?" I liken Dubai to the city on the Jetsons. An industrious city, filled with high-rises and busy highways. The only things missing were flying cars. I wasn't comfortable walking to the liquor store in a foreign place without direction, guidance or SIDEWALKS! But he insisted. As we walked, I started to retract. I got quiet. Multiple times, I'd asked him to turn around. I pleaded with him, telling him that I wasn't comfortable. He insisted that we stay the course. As we walked, our paths became darker and the distance between us got longer. I fell further behind him. He stopped here and there so that I could catch up, only for the pattern to start all over again. He knew that I didn't want to take the trip and that I had purposely changed my stride to let him know I didn't. And he purposely kept his stride to let me know that we were going to do what he wanted to, despite my opposition. I remember thinking, "He doesn't care about me." "He only cares about proving that he can walk to the liquor store in a foreign country, giving him bragging rights about how much of an adventurer he is." All the while, his newly found love is walking behind him, frightened. Suddenly, the trust and security I thought I had was gone. The peace I'd claimed months prior, as justification to change my entire life around, had suddenly faded. I felt empty. I was hurt.

By the time we got back to the hotel, I'd shut down. I didn't want to talk or sleep next to him. I gave him the silent treatment. You know the thing some of us do to get people's attention, making them aware that they'd offended us. Cut off communication when you clearly need to speak up. I've responded this way countless times. It's a natural response for me. You do something to me; I stop speaking to you. Speaks volumes, right? Pun intended. He wasn't the type to "kiss ass" to get you to talk, though. If you were mad and decided not to communicate, that was your problem, not his. You would need to get over it and move on. Meanwhile, he's taking note of your response to use it against you in the next disagreement. (This is what I eventually learned about him.)

I eventually grew tired of being silent and he was fixed in position to not respond to my response. He was clearly better at this than me. So, because I'm a pleaser and an anxious attachment type, I decided to break silence for both of us. My first thought, "give him head." (Adrian, you and my grandchildren skip this part.). We're both lying in bed, and I venture off under the covers, pull his underwear down and start to kiss the head of his dick. As I kiss, I caress his shaft and eventually take him into my mouth. He begins to pulsate and rise at the same time. He was aroused but I didn't notice any other signs of enjoyment. No moaning, groaning, touching himself or me. He just lied there, as if he were asleep. But he wasn't. He was intentionally not engaging as a way of payback for my silent treatment. So, I stopped, crawled up to my space in the bed and eventually fell asleep.

The next morning, he'd softened up enough to talk about situation. He insisted that he did nothing wrong, that he didn't understand my feelings about safety and that I was exaggerating. He also commented that the incident caused him to question his trust for me. Me silencing myself was concerning. Anxiety immediately settled-in my head, my chest and my belly. I felt as if I was no longer good enough. The impending doom of discard was creeping into my mind and heart. "He's gonna leave me", I thought. I had to do something to fix this.

I sat on his lap, with my legs wrapped around his waist, and apologized. I told him that he could trust me. I also told him that I was committed to working on my response and would be more mature about communicating my disagreements with him. I told him how much I loved and wanted to be with him.

He never apologized.

Over the life of our relationship, these patterns continued. He would silently offend and pretend he wasn't offensive; gaslighting me into thinking I was the problem. I would then, take responsibility, apologize and wait until the next opportunity to do it again.

Shortly after the Dubai trip, we had another argument, and another and another. I don't think I'd been in Texas for 2 months without arguing at least twice a month about something. Our argument wasn't about the subject of the argument. The arguments were about what we needed from each other, but the history of our lives kept us from fulfilling those needs. Our life histories shaped our personalities and showed up in how we thought about and responded in life (and each other). The arguments were never about the arguments. They were about us individually and how we couldn't partner because the individuals kept showing up. Eventually, contempt built. And we continued in a contemptuous relationship for 3 years.

I think I posed a threat to Otunde. I was strong. I had my own mind. I could make decisions without needing to lean on him at all. Some may argue the need to quiet those parts of my character, to make him feel like a man-not to emasculate him. And I'm here to say that I tried, but his treatment caused the individual me to keep showing up. I was already carrying decades of hurt. And the more he hurt me, the more my individual showed up. The individual that appeared as a formidable woman that didn't need him for anything. My individual did not pair with his individual.

CHAPTER 12:

WE FOUGHT

We fought and I still bought a house using my entire retirement from Jackson. He didn't pay a thing.

We fought and I allowed him to live bill-free in a house that he lived in. He pretended to be selling his house. He never did.

We fought and I continued to be engaged to him. He gave me the ring but never questioned when we would get married.

We fought and I continued to let him back in. I put him out. I wanted him back. He moved out. He came back.

We fought and I begged him to see me. He never did. He only saw resistance and disrespect. He saw a man, not a woman. He saw masculinity, not femininity. He saw a husband, not a wife. He saw disdain, not admiration.

Right after we'd gotten married, we started house hunting. Otunde was pressed to get out of apartment living and expressed his urgency through complaints about the apartment we lived in. "The place is too small." "There's no privacy." "The neighbors make too much noise." "They broke in my truck." While these may seem like valid grumblings, these circumstances were a "given" when living in an apartment.

We searched high and low for a new home across the entire Dallas-Ft. Worth (DFW) metroplex. Our "must haves" were different, as well as our design taste. He didn't mind an old "fixer-upper" if it came with acreage. The only problem was that he was lazy. So, I would end up "fixing" the place on my own-finances and labor. And I would be responsible for maintaining the land he was so enamored by. The same thing happened with our house in Houston. It needed major interior painting. I opted to pay someone to do the job. He insisted on a DIY. The DIY turned into CDIY. I bought the paint and supplies, prepared the rooms and painted ceilings, crown molding (that was present throughout the house), walls and baseboards. All while he lied in bed, scrolling Instagram and watched football. When I asked why he didn't help me, he said that he didn't like painting. "Well, I'll be damned, I guess I do", I responded.

I was inflexible when it came to the number of living spaces, living rooms, family rooms, formal dining areas, etc... I needed them all. I never liked the idea of combining the formal living room and the family room. The latter is where everyone gathers to watch television, entertain and lounge. The formal area is where you sat poshly with visitors while showing off your expensive ass furniture and your bomb-ass decorative skills. All while crossing your legs and pretending to pay attention to the very boring conversation. I feel the same way about formal and informal dining spaces.

We settled on a place in Arlington, Texas-close to the AT&T stadium, home of the Dallas Cowboys. The house had much more of my "must haves" than his. It was an older home but had been totally updated, except for the carpet in the spare bedrooms. And the backyard! It was spacious, with plenty of room for outdoor living and dining. The previous owners had installed a brick fence to protect the property from the lake that flowed just steps away from it. It was beautiful.

We closed on the house in April of 2022-only two months after we'd gotten married. I remember sitting at the table of the title company thinking, "What have I gotten myself into?" I didn't want the responsibility of a home that soon. The house we left behind in Houston, had worn me out. We lived in it. But I was responsible for it-mortgage, upkeep, and maintenance. This time, Otunde took on the responsibility of securing the realtor, mortgager and homeowner's insurance, but ended up getting us into a conventional mortgage, which required a large down payment with a high-interest rate. It was significantly higher than the rate I'd been able to get 2 years prior. I wanted to secure our loan through the mortgage company I'd used for my last two homes-PennyMac, hoping my borrowing history could secure a lower interest rate. But I knew better than to make such a suggestion. Lending my input would have triggered Otunde's insecurities, causing him to feel emasculated and restart a cycle of arguments I was not interested in. The ones where he would defend his insecurities and ignore any sensibility in my concerns. The ones that started in Dubai when he insisted on walking to the liquor store. So, I settled on what he wanted. A half a million-dollar home with a loan interest rate of 4.5% and a mortgage only I could manage, if push came to shove. Which it eventually did.

I tried my hardest to communicate my concerns. I told Otunde how the decision to buy didn't feel right and how our current decisions reminded me of our past ones. I remember Otunde saying once, during an argument about responsibilities in the Houston house, "I didn't want this house, you did." Which was an escape tactic for him when my callouts about his lack of engagement and interest got to be too much. When he knew I was right, he needed a way to turn the conversation down a path where he could argue his unspoken (until the argument) thoughts. The tables had turned. Now I didn't want the house. The only difference was I told him I wasn't ready.

The toxic antagonism in our relationship was palpable.

This is what it was like sharing a home with Otunde:

Watering the lawn-

Him-"The water is killing the grass."

Me-"Isn't this the same water you brush your teeth and wash your ass with?" Meanwhile, Otunde did yard work once in the 2 years we lived in the house.

Pool-

Him- "We can clean the pool ourselves." But only cleaned it once.

Me- "I'll just pay for a service to maintain the pool." Him-crickets, while my checking account is debited bi-weekly.

Gutters-

Him- "We don't need gutters." Meanwhile, pools of water are being poured close to the foundation of the house as well as the front porch.

Me-Secure gutter installation service.

Him- "You went and got those people to put those gutters in, they didn't do a good job."

Me- "Fuck You".

Drywall (after discovering termite infestation)-

Me- "The contractors are charging 2K to install a new drywall."

Him- "I can do that myself. I installed all the fucking drywall in my house in Atlanta."

Me- "So how long will this take because you've been living in your prior house for two years and still missing kitchen cabinets that you tore out, have not finished the flooring you started installing and neither have you finished painting."

Me-Pay contractor to install drywall and paint the entire dining room myself.

Him-Criticize the work during an argument.

Because Otunde was lazy and an extreme procrastinator, home purchasing and maintenance with him brought out the individual in me. In retrospect, I believe this was a manifestation of self-doubt. He would start out a task with excitement. Ready. Focused. Then mid-stream, he'd resort to, "I don't need to do all of that." "That's too much work." "I'll do it later." Or tell me what I shouldn't or couldn't do. He seemed to be boxed in by the little, skinny dark-skinned boy, with the funny name that his classmates would pick on. The little boy that was birthed by an African woman who didn't have time to confirm or affirm him because she was busy working, keeping him and his sister out of homeless shelters and off the street; all while his father was absent literally and figuratively. I thought I could help. Fill his voids. I would remind him of my move to Texas and that I did so that we could spend the rest of our lives together. 35 years, I would say. That's how much longer we had. I would also encourage him. Tell him how intelligent and skilled he was. (He truly could do anything without much thought about it.) I would also tell him how handsome he was. How I loved the tone of his skin, his beard, the shape of his hands and chest. But to him, I looked like the world that rejected him long ago. (Because the individual me kept showing up.) And he projected his feelings about them and himself onto me. He would torture me with the manifestations of my individualism, "You didn't move here for me." You moved here 'cause that's what you wanted to do." "You only do what you want to do." As if the freedom and fearlessness I had in deciding was a problem. And as if my decision, still, didn't involve him. Yes, it was what I wanted for you, and for us. As far as he was concerned, he was alone.

Things had gotten so bad between Otunde and me that I looked for an attorney. Yep. Exactly three months after I'd married this man, I went to Google and typed in, "attorneys near me" and contacted the first option that appeared in my search. Immediately, I got a response that included calendar openings for a touch-base conversation. But I froze. I wasn't ready. I kept the contact though.

CHAPTER 13:

BROKEN

During a recent conversation, I talked about how much of a force I am. I take up space quickly. My energy, posture and light present and invade like the sun in a cloudless sky. You look up and I'm there. It's immediately noticeable and engaging. I also know how my force affects people. Some leave feeling powerful, inspired and happy, while others leave feeling triggered, insecure and offended. The latter looks to tear me down. Make me less powerful. Break me like a horse. All to control the sense of demotion they feel when in a space with me. I believe Otunde experienced both. When we first met, he felt happy, loved, and overwhelmed with joy. But as our relationship progressed, and we got to experience each other more. Our individual selves. I would say he experienced more offence and dismissal, causing him to defend and retract.

Otunde was away for work for about a week. While away, I noticed his attitude being a little untoward. He was unavailable for calls at night, and when I'd query him about his whereabouts, he would become defensive and deflective. He would offer excuses for a teenager. "I was asleep." "I didn't see you calling." Given our history, I chalked it up to normalcy and kept it moving.

He was due back on a Friday but missed his flight. So, he returned home the following Monday. We'd planned to finish moving into our new home. Yeah, the one I didn't want to move into because it would only prove how much more disastrous our union was.

I pick him up. He gets in the car, kisses me on the cheek and proceeds with a phone conversation with his auntie. Because we had just moved, I wasn't sure of my whereabouts, so I let Google Maps direct me to our new residence. I exited the highway and opted for the left lane (of the two) that would lead us home. Otunde, while still on the phone, beckons me to get into the right lane. Why? I don't know. I already had a guide, so I wasn't sure why these efforts needed to be duplicated. I proceeded in the direction of the phone voice. He ended the conversation with his auntie and appeared to be agitated. I could tell by his energy. I ask, "What's the matter with you?" "I guess you have an attitude because I didn't do exactly what you asked me to?". Otunde pulled out his air pods, stuck them in each ear and proceeded to bob his head, listening to music, ignoring me. This was normal behavior. My queries about his actions made him extremely uncomfortable. They triggered him-causing him to feel angry. He would then discard me by ignoring me, turning the tables, as if I'd done something wrong. We were married, so our oscillating behaviors caused a great deal of stress and fear. More than before we got married. Before the "I dos", I could leave. Our relationship had not been sanctioned by law yet. Now we were legally bound and our failure to resolve matters could cost us emotionally, financially and proprietorially-which quadrupled the feelings of emotional loss. I'd already felt it. I'd lost tens of thousands of dollars in my move to Texas and in purchasing the house in Houston, and again, in this new house. A house that I barely wanted. A house that was purchased in contempt and that brought out the individuals in the both of us. I didn't know how much more I could take. The circumstances of our relationship were dire.

I'd brought some things from the apartment to settle in the house. I hated moving, so I took advantage of every opportunity to move items from one place to the other. Otunde wanted to survey the house. It wasn't that he hadn't already been there. It was just his way. Anytime he had something new, he was enamored with it. He loved looking at it, playing with it and learning it. His initial engagement was unmatched. But he would eventually become disinterested and discard the new thing like old, refrigerated food.

I was once his new thing.

As I unloaded the car, I continued to try and engage Otunde in conversation. He ignored me. I pleaded for honest, open conversation about what was going on with him and why he refused to talk. I told him that I didn't want our relationship to continue in the manner it had been. He ignored me.

We got back into the car and were on the way to meet friends that would help him finish our move. They were moving the big stuff-bedroom sets, sofas, and tables. I, again, attempt to engage Otunde in conversation. He placed his air pods back in his ears.

As I was making a left turn, I took my right hand and reached over to remove the air pod from Otunde's right ear. He grabbed my hand, viciously, and yelled, "Get your fucking hands off my shit." And then yelled, "Oh Shit!" I completed my left turn and looked down at my right arm. It was deformed. It no longer communicated with its partnering hand. He'd broken my arm. And as swiftly as I'd noticed my arm, I'd slammed on the car brakes and put the car in park. We were in the middle of a busy street on a Saturday morning. So, you can imagine the traffic of people going to the food store, Target, Starbucks or even on their way back home from the gym.

All I could do was scream. "You broke my fucking arm; you broke my fucking arm!" "I'm sorry babe." "I'm sorry." "Fuck, Fuck, Fuck!" "I fucked up", Otunde exclaimed. I grabbed my arm by its elbow to get some degree of connection. And then he attempted to grab my arm-trying to help. "Don't fucking touch me." "Don't touch me", I said. While at the same time, afraid and in disbelief. How on earth did this happen? Why did this happen, I thought as I babied my arm. Finally, all the arguing, resentment and anger came to a head. The pimple busted and revealed the pussy mess it contained. Otunde revealed his truest feelings about me. He never saw me as a woman. He never saw me as his wife. He never saw me as a partner. I was an adversary. An enemy. A competitor. A niggah he'd been beefing with for three years. And he finally got to whoop my ass-literally and figuratively. He finally got me to listen.

As we sat in the car, in the middle of the road, an onlooker stopped to help. Otunde wanted to drive me to the hospital. I refused. I didn't want him to take me anywhere. I asked the onlooker to call an ambulance. The ambulance arrived and the emergency technicians assisted me to the back of the truck, then into the truck, and onto the stretcher. I continued to baby my arm. The technicians asked me what happened. I offered an explanation I think most women in this circumstance offer-a lie. I told the technician that my husband and I got into a disagreement, he grabbed my arm but didn't mean to break it. They continued with their queries. And I continued with the same explanation. It was an accident. I'd gotten so frustrated with the probing, I screamed, "Whatever the fuck my husband told you is what happened. Now get me to the damn hospital." I gathered they were coercing me into a statement that would get Otunde arrested. I refused to give in to them. Then, I noticed, they hadn't immobilized my arm. I became furious. I asked, with a stern tone and full attitude, "Are you going to put my arm in a sling?" They, then, noticed me and not the drama of the situation, and proceeded to cradle my elbow and lower right arm in a thin, cotton piece of material, using its long ends to wrap around my neck, securing the make-shift sling. I continued babying my arm.

Then the cops show up, asking the same questions. "Ma'am, what happened to your arm?" "Is that man your husband", pointing in the way that Otunde was standing. "Yes, he's my husband", I respond. "So can you tell me what happened to your arm?" "Your husband told me, but I want to get a statement from you", said the police officer. "Whatever he told you is what happened", I responded. "Can y'all take me to the hospital?" "If you hadn't noticed, my arm is in two and I need to get it taken care of." "You all seem more interested in taking my husband to jail than getting me medical assistance", I exclaim again. The officers eventually went away, and I was taken to the nearby hospital's emergency room.

I never pressed charges. And we didn't separate. Well, not immediately. We moved into our house and on with our lives. I wasn't ready to leave him. Nor could I. Aside from my girlfriends who lived an hour away, he was all that I knew in Dallas. And my arm would not be healed for another 6 months. So, I wasn't in a place where I could tell him to get the fuck out or take care of myself. I did what I did best. I Moved on.

I also felt the need to protect Otunde. He'd already been to jail, twice, for domestic violence. Yep. You read it right. I knew it and always wondered if I would ever be a victim of his past crimes. He'd offered details of his past experiences. Once with his ex-wife. She cheated and he broke into their house and choked the shit out of her. The second incident involved a girlfriend that made negative comments about his mother. He choked her too.

Otunde's domestic violence history was not a deal breaker for me. As a part of probation, for his prior incidents, he had to complete domestic violence and anger management courses. Often, he would refer to the "pearls" of those courses-making me believe he had worked through the issues that would trigger such responses. But that was a lie. Me lying to myself. He'd been raged with me numerous times before my arm popped in two. So, I knew it was always there. The part of him that resented me. The part of him that hated me so much that he would hurt me emotionally, mentally, and now, physically. The part of him that hated himself, his mother and father, now was projected onto me.

I'd seen my father beat the shit out of my mother. Routinely. He'd climb through windows and even removed windowpanes to get to her. I was young, so I couldn't put any of what I witnessed into context. I didn't understand anything but my mother taking the licks of my father's fist. This would happen often, but they would stay together. And, days after their fights, I would hear them making love. She never broke up with him. We never moved. She stayed. We stayed. She willingly let him abuse her emotionally, mentally and physically. Like I did with Otunde. The circumstances of my life made sense.

What I didn't realized in my ripe age is what I was being conditioned to-abuse, neglect, abandonment, and disrespect from people that said, "I love you." I was being conditioned to accept dysfunctional and unhealthy behavior from people that were supposed to protect, guide and affirm me. And unbeknownst to me, this conditioning silently removed standards that came naturally with healthy, functioning behavior and relationships. The standards that were created when you witnessed your parents say, "I love you", and treat each other with love through respect, acknowledgement, and self-accountability. The standards that were created when your mother responded healthily to disrespect by not tolerating it and protecting her children. The standards that were created when you witness your father holding your mother and not slapping her. The standards that were created when the lovemaking you heard was love and not toxicity.

Stuck

Stuck is where my choice of men came from-stuck in the hurt of my father. The man who was domineering, callous and abusive, but also the man who provided me shelter, food and a degree of protection. So, no matter how I've spoken about my worst romantic relationships, I willingly participated because I was still a little girl, in The City, with Babalu. I was right at home with them, feeling like I was with my daddy being neglected, controlled, and abused. Feeling right at home, meeting their needs, despite their explicit neglect of mine. While the relationships were occurring in real-time, my responses to the experiences were occurring in past time. It was like travelling back 30 years while standing in the now. Otunde would make a comment that triggered 12-year-old Charkes being neglected by her daddy and adult Charkes would respond to him as an adult would, but with the hurt of a child.

Where I Was

Stuck is where my choices as a woman came from. I've been held hostage, mentally and emotionally, by the woman that birthed me, then abused and neglected me. The woman that I remember walking me to school, showing up for lunch to give me a majorette baton and putting my hair in two puffs for school pictures. The woman that I look so much like. I'm stuck in the last time she beat me because my dad beat her. I'm stuck when she left me alone, in the middle of the living room floor, going to start her "pissing" session with my dad, at The Banana Boat. I'm stuck in the time I noticed her giving up on herself. When she stopped smiling. When she stopped wearing hot pants. When she stopped wearing lipstick on her lips and cheeks. When she would just sit and stare for hours, disconnected from reality. Disconnected from the 8 children that she once carried and brought forth. I'm stuck in the time I saw her sitting on a crate, at the back of the laundromat, in layers of clothes and adorned in make-shift jewelry. Still staring. Disconnected. From us. I'm stuck in the time I realized she was homeless.

In my 40's, I'm still that little girl, sitting in the middle of the floor, waiting for her mother to come back. I'm still that little girl waiting for her parents to rescue her from the monsters that molested her while in foster care. I'm still that little girl yearning for her parents to tell her that she's more than "a responsible child". I'm still that little girl wanting to turn back time so that her parents can attend her graduations and dance recitals together. I'm still that little girl who wants her parents to stop fighting. I want my daddy to stop beating my mommy. I want my mommy to be strong enough to leave him and take care of herself and us. I want her to show me how to be me.

LAST HURT

I understand love and hurt occurring at the same time. I understand them synonymously. But I don't understand which came first. Did my parents' hurt bind them and did love follow? Were they ever in love? Or were they just two pained people who misinterpreted their emotions? Did they ever love me and my siblings? Both my heart and brain query each other, waiting for one or the other to respond. And even when my brain seems to have the right answer, the feeling of dissonance in my heart causes continued examination. So, no matter how I spoke of the people and occurrences of my life, I was responding from places that I'd been and seen before. The places that hurt me first.

Life was changing for me. In less than a year, I'd gotten married, broken my arm, lost my brother, my job, my man and my mind. I was literally, breaking down. Otunude was no longer attentive. I was wondering how we would pay our bills, all while grieving the loss of my brother and myself. I'd cry often, wondering how I'd gotten to such a lowly place. I no longer recognized myself nor my life. Life wasn't life, at all. It felt like hell. Like the time my siblings and I were taken to a group home. It was a temporary means of living until social services could find a permanent home for us. I was placed on the first floor to sleep, and I remember hearing the voice of a boy. He was mumbling and grinding his teeth. I got up from my bed to confirm what I'd heard and what my eyes saw was more than expected. The boy was lying in a crib, contracted, drooling and seemingly uncomfortable. He looked to be past the age of a child that should have been in a crib. But I imagine the crib being the safest place for him. It confined him. He couldn't fall out and hurt himself. I stood and stared at him for a while. I wondered if his mumbling was due to pain or if it was due to his disability. If it were due to pain, he felt the same way I did. The only difference was the way we communicated. He mumbled and I cried. My relationship with Otunde felt like the boy in the crib.

I had to leave.

I secured a travel assignment two hours away from Arlington. In East Texas where Matthew McConaughey grew up. I'd never taken this approach to work before, but it was all that was available, in the time I needed. Although my pay was significantly less than before, it was enough to pay my bills. And I could start sooner than I would with a permanent job. So, I took it.

By this time, Otunde and I were not communicating. My housing quarters was our living room and I slept on the sofa. I did not feel connected to him or our relationship. He'd finally proven to me that he didn't have the capacity to love me the way I needed to be loved. Or maybe I was seeing him in real-time. Not in the places of "stuck" that would usually cause me to overlook his character and the predicament of our relationship. He remained callus and unconcerned, despite the loss I'd experienced and expressed. He didn't ask questions. And when I asked about his lack of interest, his reply was, "If you want me to know something, you will tell me." I wasn't surprised though. He never asked questions, even at the beginning of our relationship. But my spirit was different, causing my will to change. Over the three years of our relationship, my will had been dampened by Otunde's domineering character. By his refusal to see me. By his continuous labelling and discard. Now the dampening behavior had lost its effect, and I began to feel a new energy.

The time had come for me to report for my assignment. I eagerly packed. I was getting ready for what I knew would be my new life. Like I had 30 years ago, when I left for Cookman. An awakening was coming on and I was looking to find me again. I was looking forward to the feeling Celie had when she left Mister (when Fantasia played her).

> *"I'm gohhnnnaaahh, take a deep breath, I'm gonna hold my head and put my shoulders back and look you straight in the eye. I'm gonna flirt with somebody, whe they walk by. I'm gonna sing out. Sing Out."*

Otunde wasn't aware of the details of my assignment. I didn't share them because he didn't ask, and I didn't want him to know. Boundary setting had begun. The Uber pulled up and I grabbed my luggage, despite my still weak, right arm. Otunde attempted to help, but I insisted on him not. I didn't want any part of him. I didn't want the slightest connection. I didn't want anything that would evoke emotion, distracting me from what I needed- to get away from his ass. I got into the back seat of the Uber and didn't say a word. I didn't say goodbye, I love you or see you later. I just seated myself, secured my seatbelt and looked straight ahead.

The short two-hour drive was long. Long as hell. I cried, screamed, and thought. And cried again. The only question running a marathon in my head was, "Why?" "Why was this happening?" "Why didn't Otunde love me?" "Why was he the way he was?" "Why had he disappointed me so much?" I called his aunt on the way there and shared where I was in relationship, marriage and life. She and her husband were super close, so naturally, he listened in on our conversation. He posed the following question, "Do you want the relationship?" He went on to say that he was willing to speak to Otunde, but wouldn't if he didn't want the relationship. My answer was, "Yes." "Yes", I wanted the relationship. "Yes", I wanted to continue what had begun as a fairy tale. I wanted to continue love and being in love but felt hopeless when I thought of who I wanted this love with. My mind checked my heart. There I was crying and saying yes, again, to what I didn't need. **(STUCK)**

Upon arrival, I messaged Otunde, letting him know that I'd gotten there safely. His response was a "thumbs up" on my message.

A week went by, then two, then three, then a month. Otunde never asked where I was, where I was working, where I was living or if I was ok. He never came for me. The feelings of neglect and abuse had deepened. **(STUCK)** I was still his wife. And I was more than 2 hours away in an unfamiliar place. He never even reached out to see if I was ok. I had all the answers I needed. It was time to finalize my "move on", so I called my attorney and resurrected my divorce filing.

Recently, I heard a sermon by Sarah Jakes Roberts about "Missing the Moment". As she unpacked this message, she illustrated the ways in which God creates pathways to our greatness. How He constructs life experiences for us to learn, develop and succeed. He does this by aligning these experiences with the most underdeveloped parts of us. The areas where we lack in romantic relationships, careers, and family. The areas that become our achilles heels. They are the times where we were first hurt. When mommy died and you ran at the first sight of love again, for fear of loss and abandonment. Or when daddy left your mother and left you at the same time. And now, you can't connect with your own children. Or when your mother beat the shit out of you and now you verbally and physically abuse your children. The hurt keeps hurting. It cycles and recycles. Until "The Moment".

My relationship with Otunde led to "The Moment" for me. No, it wasn't the arguing, the breaking of my arm or the divorce. It was how broken my spirit was and how disconnected I'd become from God, and therefore, myself. It was how I wasn't thriving physically, emotionally, financially or creatively. I'd gained a significant amount of weight; I'd started having vertigo spells and my dominant arm was broken. I no longer had a retirement, and I was in debt from a wedding that occurred only a year before writing these words. I wasn't writing. My moment occurred when I realized how he brought out the very worst in me. Being with Otunde made me defensive and depressed. Being with him also made me angry at times. Being with him caused counter-responses that that were outrageous. I'd get so frustrated that I'd throw things at him, scream at the top of my lungs and break things. Being with him reminded me of the worst times in my life and the worst parts of myself. Like being at home with my dad, or in the group home with the boy in the crib or when my dad would beat my mom. I'd finally had my "Moment".

Sarah Jakes Roberts also speaks in a sermon about "Form". She talked about how we all arrive in the way God meant for us to be. Not only physically, but also in spirit. As life happens to us, we begin to build upon that form. We add to it. The additions are responses to life events-tragedy, loss and rejection-which show up as depression, anger, resentment. With every life occurrence, we look to replace our natural beings with coats of protection that don't represent our true selves. Copping, adaptation, secrets, wall-building, seclusion, addiction and abuse all serve to protect our inner beings from the insults of life. These coats of arms defend our inner selves. Our form. They are intertwined with reminders of what happened in the past and as soon as history repeats itself, the layers report for duty. Protecting and defending. And if you've suffered varying insults, your layers follow suit. You can carry many coats. You're angry, depressed and abusive because your mother beat you and your father abandoned you. Or you're dependent, anxious and pessimistic for the same reasons. And this is how you show up in the world, in your personal lives, in your career and to God. Eventually, there will come a time when the layers of your coats create so much distance between you and your true form that you lose yourself. You stop feeling, loving, seeing, and hoping. You become your coat. It's like a callus on the heel of your foot. Its thickness represents initial and continuous insults, causing numbness. So much that you can't feel your heel anymore. You just feel skin. The responses to insults.

While in East Texas, I had another moment. I realized that my achilles heel was not Otunde, but the disconnections with my mother and father. This attracted me to Otunde and caused me to remain in our contemptuous relationship. Me and Otunde's relationship not only mimicked that of my parents, but also represented what I wanted to restore with them together and individually. With Otunde, I was looking to repair the connections that were interrupted by my parents' mis-shappened lives. I was looking to fill gaps of love, belonging, and acceptance that were left behind when Ya-Yow first left me home alone and when I first noticed Babalu never being home. I was looking for them in him and the many other romantic relationships I'd been in. I was stuck where I was last hurt.

I'm aware now. This book, initially, was merely a continuance of my life's journey. I wanted to log, depict, and illustrate so that someone like me can know that they are human like me. And so that same someone completes this reading feeling inspired and empowered; understanding their worse circumstance does not have to be their final one. But as I lived, my intentions for this book changed. As I lived in the layers, I became weighted and uncomfortable. I wanted them off. I wanted to get back to my truest form. I wanted and needed to get back to me. And to do that, I had to shed. This book is my shedding. The depictions, situations, events, relationships and revelations are me ridding myself of all that's not natural. Writing this book has allowed me to understand how the sheets of protection distanced me from myself. It revealed how most people experience me and I no longer want those impressions to be lasting ones.

I left Otunde more than a year ago and we have finally divorced. Since then, I've grown. By shedding, I'm learning what my boundaries are and how to set standards accordingly. I am aware. Extremely aware. I know my light and strengths and how they affect people. Differently. I'm aware of the cues that drive me engagement and disengagement. I know that love and tolerance have limits and that my love is limitless, but my tolerance is not. I can love you and leave you. And still love you. I know that I must always align with my true form and anything and anyone that disrupts that alignment cannot be a part of my journey. I know that if I am attracted to and engage in any degree of relationship with hurt, I am still hurt. I know that I am light. I know that I am loved. I know that I am no no longer STUCK!

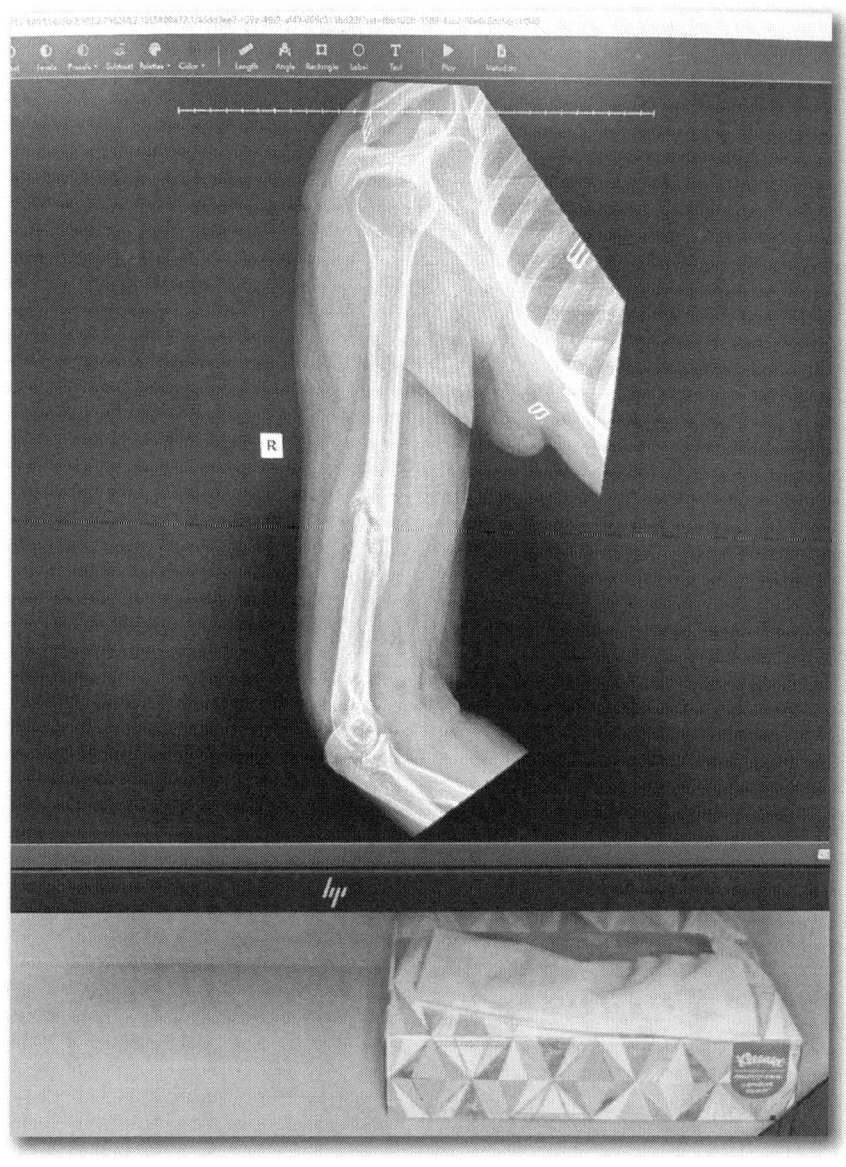

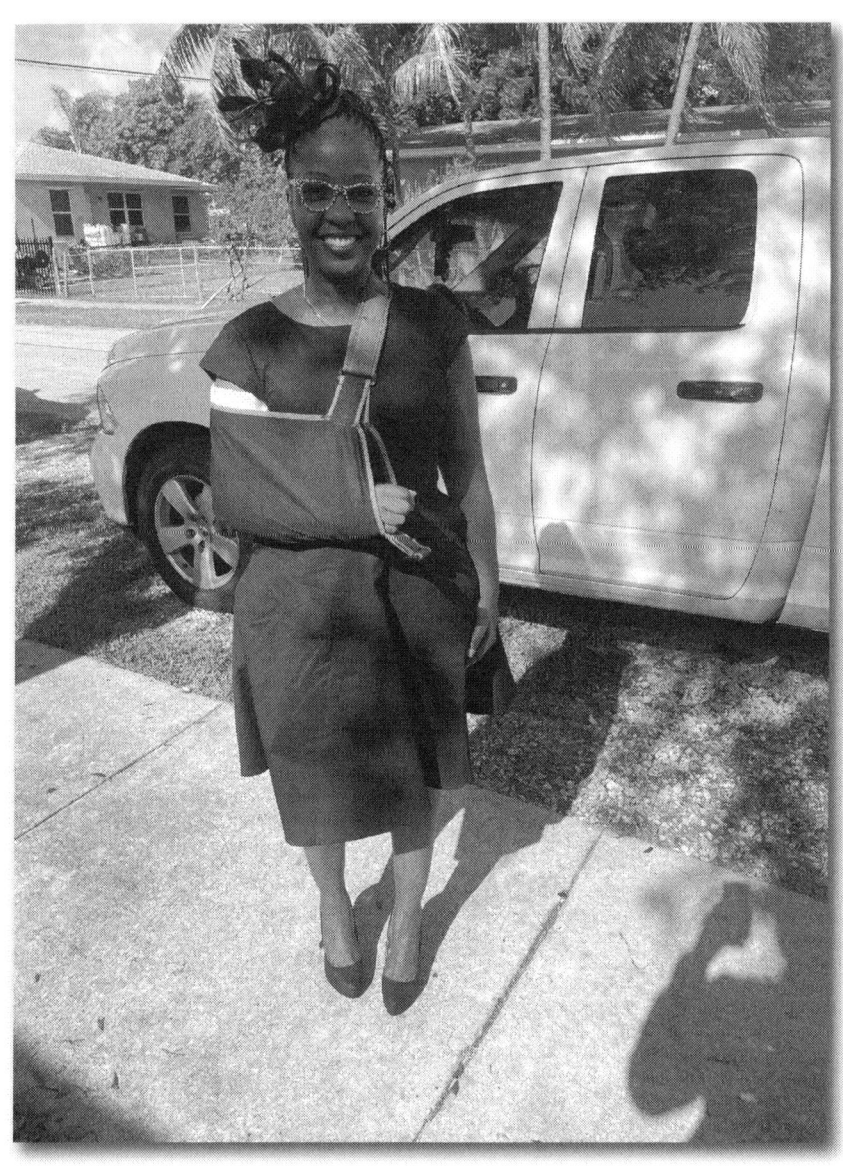

Made in the USA
Monee, IL
09 September 2024

65418615R00085